Abel
20.60

20.00 ℰℭ/2

D1498231

DISCARDED

THE
UNIVERSITY OF WINNIPEG
PORTAGE & BALMORAL
WINNIPEG 2, MAN.   CANADA

JOHN HEYWOOD

Entertainer

A REPUTED PORTRAIT OF JOHN HEYWOOD

PR
2566
·D4
1937a

JOHN HEYWOOD
Entertainer

BY

R. de la BÈRE

M. A., F. R. HIST. S.

*Professor at the Royal Air Force
College, Cranwell, Lincolnshire*

Folcroft Library Editions */1970*

Limited to 150 Copies

JOHN HEYWOOD
Entertainer

BY

R. de la BÈRE
M. A., F. R. HIST. S.

*Professor at the Royal Air Force
College, Cranwell, Lincolnshire*

LONDON
GEORGE ALLEN & UNWIN LTD
MUSEUM STREET

FIRST PUBLISHED IN 1937

All rights reserved

PRINTED IN GREAT BRITAIN BY
UNWIN BROTHERS LTD., WOKING

Art thou Heywood with the mad mery wit
Ye forsooth maister that same is euen hit
Art thou Heywood that applieth mirth more then thrift
Ye sir I take mery mirth a golden gift
Art thou Heywood that hath made many mad plaies
Ye many plaies fewe good woorkes in all my daies
Art thou Heywood that hath made men mery long
Ye and will if I be made mery among
Art thou Heywood that woulde be made mery now
Ye sir helpe me to it now I beseche yow

matris
in piam memoriam

CONTENTS

THE PEDIGREE OF JOHN HEYWOOD

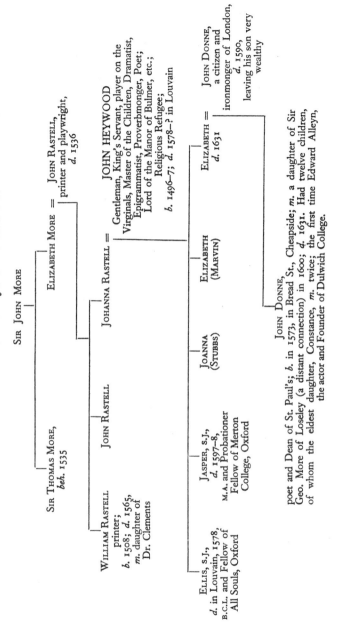

Sir John More

Sir Thomas More, *beh.* 1535 | John Rastell | Elizabeth More = John Rastell, printer and playwright, *d.* 1536

Johanna Rastell = John Heywood, Gentleman, King's Servant, player on the Virginals, Master of the Children, Dramatist, Epigrammatist, Proverbmonger, Poet; Lord of the Manor of Bulmer, etc.; Religious Refugee; *b.* 1496–7; *d.* 1578–? in Louvain

William Rastell, printer; *b.* 1508; *d.* 1565; *m.* daughter of Dr. Clements

Elizabeth, *d.* 1631 = John Donne, a citizen and ironmonger of London, *d.* 1590, leaving his son very wealthy

Ellis, S.J., *d.* in Louvain, 1578, B.C.L. and Fellow of All Souls, Oxford | Jasper, S.J., *d.* 1597–8, M.A. and Probationer Fellow of Merton College, Oxford | Joanna (Stubbs) | Elizabeth (Marvin)

John Donne, poet and Dean of St. Paul's; *b.* in 1573, in Bread St., Cheapside; *m.* a daughter of Sir Geo. More of Loseley (a distant connection) in 1600; *d.* 1631. Had twelve children, of whom the eldest daughter, Constance, *m.* twice; the first time Edward Alleyn, the actor and Founder of Dulwich College.

BIBLIOGRAPHY

FOR THE STUDY OF JOHN HEYWOOD'S WORKS

BALE, Bishop John. *Index Britanniae Scriptorum quos ex variis biblio-
thecis non parvo labore collegit Ioannes Baleus, cum aliis.* Ed. Reginald
Lane Poole and Mary Bateson. Oxford, 1902.

 *Scriptorum illustrium Maioris Brytannie, quam nunc Angliam &
Scotiam uocant; Catalogus . . . Basileae, apud I. Oporinum*, 1557-9.
2 vols.

BANG, W. *Acta Anglo-Lovaniensia; John Heywood und sein Kreis.* Englishe
Studien, band 38, 1907.

BASTARD, Thomas. *Chrestoleros; Seven Bookes of Epigrams,* 1598. Spenser
Society, 1888.

BEDIER, Joseph. *Les Fabliaux*, 2nd ed. Paris, 1895.

BOLWELL, Robert G. W. *Life and Works of John Heywood.* Columbia
University Studies, New York, 1921.

BRANDL, Alois. *Quellen des Weltlichen Dramas in England vor Shake‾
speare.* Strassburg, 1898.

Cambridge History of English Literature. Ed. A. W. Ward and A. R.
Waller, 14 vols. New York and London, 1907 ff.

CAMDEN, William. *Remains Concerning Britain, with Memoir by Thomas
Moule.* London, 1870.

 Annales Rerum Anglicarum et Hibernicarum, etc. Ed. Thos.
Hearn. 3 vols. 1717.

CHAMBERS, E. K. *The Mediaeval Stage.* 2 vols. Oxford, 1903.

 Notes on the History of the Revels Office under the Tudors.
London, 1906.

COLLIER, John Payne. *The History of English Dramatic Poetry, and the
Annals of the Stage.* 3 vols. London, 1831.

DODSLEY, Robert. *A Select Collection of Old Plays.* Ed. Isaac Reed,
Octavius Gilchrist, and John Payne Collier. London, 1825.

DUFF, E. Gordon. *The Printers, Stationers and Bookbinders of Westminster and London from 1476 to 1535.* Cambridge, 1906.

— *Fabliaux et contes des poètes français des XIe, XIIe, XIIIe, XIVe,
et XVe siècles.* 4 vols. Paris, 1808.

FARMER, John S. *See* under Heywood.

FOXE, John. *Acts and Monuments, etc.* 9th ed. 3 vols. London, 1684.

FULLER, Thomas. *The Church History of Britain.* Ed. J. S. Brewer. 4 vols. Oxford, 1845.
    The History of the Worthies of England. Ed. P. Austin Nuttall. 3 vols. London, 1840.

GOOGE, Barnaby. *Foure Bookes of Husbandry.* Tr. from Conrad Heresbach. London, 1601.

GRAVES, T. S. "The Heywood Circle" and "The Reformation" in *Modern Philology.* Chicago, 1913.

Harleian Miscellany, The. Ed. William Oldys and Thomas Park. 10 vols. 1808, etc.

HARINGTON, Sir John. Tr. *Ariosto, Orlando Furioso.* London, 1634.
    The Metamorphosis of Ajax, with the Anatomy and Apology, to which is added Ulysses Upon Ajax. Chiswick, 1814.

HENSLOWE, John. *Diary.* Ed. W. W. Greg. A. H. Bullen, 1908.

HEYWOOD, John. All Dramatic Works, in Tudor Facsimile Reprints. Ed. John S. Farmer.
    The Dramatic Writings of. Ed. John S. Farmer. Early English Drama Society. London, 1905.
    The Proverbs, Epigrams, and Miscellanies of. Ed. John S. Farmer. Early English Drama Society. London, 1906.
    The Spider and the Flie, and Gentleness and Nobility. Ed. John S. Farmer. Early English Drama Society. London, 1908.
    Wit and Folly. Ed. with Introduction by F. W. Fairholt. Percy Society Publications. Vol. xx, 1846.
    The Proverbs and Epigrams of. Spenser Society. Vol. I, 1867.

LANGBAINE, Gerard. *Account of the English Dramatick Poets.* Oxford, 1691.
    The Lives and Characters of the English Dramatick Poets, etc. London, 1699.

Letters and Papers, Foreign and Domestic, of the Reign of Henry VIII. Arranged and catalogued by J. S. Brewer, James Gairdner, and R. H. Brodie. London, 1862, etc.

MACHYN, Henry. *The Diary of.* Ed. John Gough Nichols. Camden Society, 1848.

MADDEN, Sir Frederick. *Privy Purse Expenses of the Princess Mary.* London, 1831.

PEACHAM, Henry. *Compleat Gentleman.* Ed. G. S. Gordon. Oxford, 1906.

PITSEUS, John. *Relationum Historicarum de Rebus Anglicis.* Paris, 1619.

POLLARD, A. W. *English Miracle Plays, Moralities, and Interludes.* 5th ed. Oxford, 1909.

PUTTENHAM, George. *See* G. G. Smith.

REDFORD, John. Brit. Mus. MSS. Additional No. 15233; containing *Wit and Science,* and short poems.

REED, Arthur W. 1. *The Canon of Heywood's Plays.* London, 1918.

2. *The Beginnings of English Secular and Romantic Drama.* London, 1922.

3. *Early Tudor Drama.* London, 1926.

4. *Utopia.* Waltham St. Lawrence, 1929.

SHARMAN, Julian. *The Proverbs of John Heywood,* with Introduction. London, 1874.

SMITH, G. Gregory. *Elizabethan Critical Essays.* 2 vols. Oxford, 1904.

State Papers, Domestic Series, of the Reigns of Edward VI, Mary, Elizabeth, 1547–80, *Calendar of.* Public Record Office, London. 1856.

State Papers, Foreign Series, of the Reign of Elizabeth, 1572–4, *Calendar of.* Ed. Allen James Crosby. London, 1876.

State Papers, Domestic Series, of the Reign of Elizabeth, Addenda, 1566–79, *Calendar of.* Ed. Mary Anne Everett Greene. London, 1871.

STOW, John. *Annales, or a Generall Chronicle of England.* London, 1631.

A Survey of London. Ed. Charles Lethbridge Kingsford. 2 vols. Oxford, 1908.

SWOBODA, Wilhelm. *John Heywood als Dramatiker.* Vienna, 1888.

SYMONDS, John Addington. *Shakespeare's Predecessors in the English Drama.*

Tottel's Miscellany. Ed. J. P. Collier. London, 1867.

WALLACE, Charles Wm. *The Children of the Chapel at Blackfriars,* 1597–1603. Univ. of Nebraska Studies, Vol. 8, No. 2, 1908.

The Evolution of the English Drama up to Shakespeare. Berlin, 1912.

WALTON, Izaak. *The Life and Death of Dr. John Donne, Late deane of St. Paul's.* 1640.

WARD, Adolphus W. *The Spider and the Flie,* by John Heywood, with Introduction. Spenser Society. 1894.

   A History of English Dramatic Literature. 3 vols. London, 1899.

WARTON, Thomas. *The History of English Poetry.* 4 vols. London, 1824.

WILSON, Thomas. *Arte of Rhetorique.* Ed. G. H. Mair. Oxford, 1907.

À WOOD, Anthony. *Athenae Oxonienses* (with the Fasti). Additions and ed. by Philip Bliss. 5 vols. London, 1813.

   Survey of the Antiquities of the City of Oxford, composed in 1661–6. Andrew Clark. Oxford Hist. Society, Oxford, 1889.

YOUNG, Karl. "The Influence of French Farce upon the plays of John Heywood." *Modern Philology,* Vol. II, 1904.

JOHN HEYWOOD—ENTERTAINER

INTRODUCTION

VOYAGES of discovery often lead men into strange byroads and quiet backwaters. We all wish to explore the unknown and to make during the narrow spell of modern life some contribution to learning, before we pass by and are no more seen. Some have the dramatic good fortune to discover new territories in the world or in the world which throbs about them. To some it is given to prise open secret tombs in Egypt, or to disentangle the cuneiform and hieroglyphic, or to unearth fossils or antique weapons.

This book deals with a humbler theme—the life and work of one who lived four centuries ago, one whose name for three centuries at least has been unknown and is still unknown to-day except to that small ascetic band who delight in painfully piecing together the jigsaw of such evidences as can be disclosed by the careful and, strangely enough, by the casual reader in the greater and rarer libraries of the world.

This book deals with the life and work of a Tudor playwright—to embrace all his versatility in one word—viz. John Heywood. The study of his life and work might be regarded as an example of the methods and quality of modern research. For twenty years scholars have explored on his behalf every avenue—as the modern jargon has it—private papers of the Tudor Court, the internal evidence of his multifarious writings, side references in contemporary authors, legal documents, inquisitions, parish and college registers, traditions; and so a shaking edifice has been built up brick by brick until as much is known about Heywood as we should like to be known about Shakespeare.

For many reasons there still must be conjecture about the

man, not least when his name can be rendered Haywoode, Heywoodde, Haywodde, Heyvode, Hayuodus, Hayward, Haiwodus, Haywod, Heywod, Heewood, Heewode, and in many other ways, including A Wod and A Wode.

I shall therefore construct his life as dogmatically as I dare from my own research and from the researches of others whose names, like that of Dr. A. W. Reed in particular, are recorded at the beginning of this book, and to whom I have paid tribute inadequately in view of the thoroughness and ingenuity of their scholarship.

John Heywood is well worthy of study. Among many claims on our attention the principal lies in his plays, which were the theme of Peacham, Fuller, Camden, and Jonson. They help us a little to understand the sudden blaze of Shakespeare's genius.

Heywood is to be correlated with John Bale, William Cornish, Thomas More, John and William Rastell, and Henry Medwall in the invention of the English non-ecclesiastical drama. He is to be regarded as the restorer to English of the Chaucerian humour which had been clogged by the bloodless abstractions of the Moralities.

But he is almost equally interesting as being a typical man of his age: a social success, a singer, a player, a wit, a dramatist. He was in intimate association with Henry VIII, Edward VI, Mary, and Elizabeth. He was even more intimate with Thomas More. He was a strong Catholic partisan, was implicated in religious plots, and nearly suffered martyrdom at the hands of Cranmer for denying the King's ecclesiastical authority: and in the end the new Elizabethan outlook on religion drove him into exile in the Low Countries, where he died, a venerated benefactor of the Society of Jesus.

He died after about eighty years of full living in the course of which he rose from being a singer and an instrumentalist to being a *generosus*, i.e. gentleman, and a lord of the manor by gift, a landowner by purchase, a member of a City company.

Whether we regard him solely as a boon companion, or solely as a playwright, he is worthy of our attention. He deserves it as a proverbmonger, as an epigrammatist, as a wit, as a poet.

And yet in the end his greatest importance may lie in the light he throws upon Tudor society and particularly upon the Tudor interpretation of humour at the table or on the stage. And the best illustration of the man is found in the author.

John Heywood was born on or about April 18, 1497. This is fixed by a letter which he wrote to Lord Burghley, in which he says that his life "can not be by all lykeliehoode aboue twoo or three yeares being nowe LXXVIII yeares of age." The letter is dated, "this XVIII of Aprell 1575," and signed "Your honors most hombell orator as he ys greately bownden, Jhon Heywood." But even if there were no signature both the matter and the manner of the letter, e.g. the incorrigible mad merry humour and the use of proverbs, would leave no doubt of the identity of the writer, whose service to his own time lay in his irrepressible sense of fun, and to all time in his restoration to English literature of the outlook of Chaucer.

Of his parentage we know nothing for certain. He was probably born in London. But there are others who assign him, with, but after, Homer, several birthplaces, and have urged the claims of North Mimms, a hamlet off the North Road not far from St. Albans in Hertfordshire; and of Stock Harvard in the Hundred of Chelmsford, and five miles south-west of it, where there are still Heywoods living to-day.

In the Appendix to this book the curious will find some of the rival evidences which have been alleged of his "home town." The perusal of these evidences may provoke others to bring up legal or literary artillery. But I cannot imagine where they will find it; certainly not in the Parish Registers, which rarely go back so far.

There is also darkness over the face of the first seventeen

years of Heywood's life. Nothing is known of them for certain, though much is guessed. Antony à Wood, writing in the seventeenth century, takes him straight on to Oxford University.

It is a plausible theory, but no more than a theory, that during his boyhood Heywood was a chorister under William Cornish, Master of the Chapel Royal. This would bring him into touch with the plays and pageants which were so popular at the Tudor Court. But he is not mentioned in the Records of the Chapel Royal; and he might with equal argument have been in Wolsey's Chapel or in St. Paul's choir, and there have attracted the attention of the King, who was wont to impound his friends' best boy actors and singers. And in 1509, when Henry ascended the throne, he would be twelve years old and just coming into good singing voice.

The theory has misled its ardent supporters in the end to assign Heywood's plays to Cornish or to Cornish's successor at the Chapel in 1525, William Crane. The spectacle of unexpected brilliance, whether it be of Homer, Isaiah, Shakespeare, and in a lesser degree of Heywood, often confounds the critics, who fall back on self-invented theories which they alone can understand, and instead of accepting the full man, as tradition has given him to us, they set to work to articulate him or abolish him, forgetful of the heights to which the human genius can rise on rare occasions.

Dr. J. S. Farmer, who has contributed more than most to the study of Heywood, is equally ardent in stressing "his University career." He considers that he probably went to Oxford at fourteen, as did Wolsey and Udall, while Heywood's son Jasper went at twelve, and his grandson John Donne at only eleven.

Antony à Wood goes on to say that "he laid a foundation of learning in this University and particularly, as it seems, in that ancient hostel called Broadgates, in St. Aldgate's Parish. But the crabbedness of Logic not suiting with his airie genie, he retired to his native place and became noted to all witty men, especially to Sir Thomas More, with whom he was very familiar, wrot several matters of poetry and was the first, as some say (but I think it false) that wrot English plays, taking opportunity thence to make notable work with the clergy. He had admirable skill also in instrumental and vocal musick, but whether he made any compositions in either I cannot find.

"Before the title" (i.e. of his allegory of *The Spider and the Flie*) "is the picture of John Heywood from head to foot, printed from a wooden cut, with a fur gown on representing the fashion of that almost belonging to a Master of Arts but the bottom of the sleeves reach no lower than his knees. On his head is a round cap, his chin and lips are closely shaved and he hath a girdle."[1]

But there is no official record of John Heywood as the College Registers of "Broadgates," or Pembroke College, as it now is called, only go back to 1570. But there is a kind of evidence that might go to corroborate Wood's statement that he was an Oxford man. For instance, he is referred to in W. Rastell's will as "Dominus," which some have construed as "graduate." Also he writes in his *Epigrammes*:

Of Verdingales.

Alas por Verdingales must lie in the streete:
To house them no doore in the city made meete:
Syns at our narrow doores they in ease can not win,
Send them to Oxford at Brodegates to get in.

and

Of Testons.

Testons be gone to Oxford, God be them spede,
To study in Brazenose there to procede.

For those who would like to blend the theories that he

[1] Indeed, Wood considers that all the woodcuts in *The Spider and the Flie* introduce the author's portrait.

was a royal chorister and that when his voice broke he went up to Oxford and stayed there till he joined the King's service again, Julian Sharman (1874) quotes attractively from the Harleian MS. XL, "and when any of these children come to be XVIII years of age and their voices change ne cannot be preferred in the chappelle their nombere being full, then, if they will assente, the kyng assignethe them to a College of Oxeford or Cambridge of his foundation, there to be at fynding stydye both suffytyantly tylle the kyng may otherwise advaunce them."

The last bit of evidence I can adduce on the matter is that Wood tells us that Heywood had several children, to whom he had given a *liberal* education. Amongst them was Ellis, "son of John Heywood, the famous epigrammatist, who was born in London and *educated at Oxford*." Also, there was Jasper, "a quaint poet in his younger days, son of John Heywood the famous epigrammatist: was born in London *and went to Oxford* at twelve in 1547." These two were for a time rather wild, "to the great grief of their father."

> Old Haywoods sons did wax so wild and youthful
> It made their aged father sad and wrathful.
> James Harington's Epigrams.

But in 1547 Ellis was elected a Fellow of All Souls, Oxford. Jasper was, we are told, a Fellow on probation at Merton College and "bare away the bell in disputations at home and in the publick schools."

Heywood's might have been, therefore, a university family, a theory to which the literary character and the contents of his work lend colour. We must pass on with not much more certainty to the Court life of Heywood and here "the Kynges Bokes of Paymentes" will be our chief authority.

Partly owing to the varied and unstabilized spelling of the day, which, in the space of a few years, could render the name in twenty different ways, we cannot always be sure in these and other papers when the dramatist or his relatives or merely namesakes are concerned.

We find on October 9, 1520, for instance, a John Heywood, a yeoman usher, receiving eightpence a day; a William Heywood, the King's Joiner employed in 1514 on the "Great Harry" and in 1521 at the Field of the Cloth of Gold, receiving twelve pence a day; John Avoodde received in December 1520 a grant for his "lyverage." In June 1530 a record appears:

Item the xxix day paied to John a Wod that kepith the King's gossehawk for his quarter wages . . . £4 11. 5.

All or any of these Heywoods may have been relatives of the playwright. One of them may have been his father; particularly the yeoman John Heywood, who retired from the active list and was pensioned at four pounds a year in 1525–6 at a time of a royal economic blizzard after the French War.

But all students of Heywood have agreed to draw attention to the State Papers of 1519–20[1] in which for Michaelmas 1519 the item occurs:

For John Haywoode Qrtor wages at xx li by the yere—100/-.

The item is repeated in the Christmas accounts, 1519; in the Easter accounts, 1520; and in the Midsummer accounts, 1520. At Michaelmas 1520 the item appears again with a qualification:

Item for John Hawwode synger wages 100/-.

It is repeated at Christmas 1520.

These are the first known records of John Heywood as a salaried official at the Court of Henry VIII. But other records may have been lost. He wrote of himself "*Longe* have I been a singinge man." If, therefore, he was not a chorister at the Chapel Royal or a gentleman of the Chapel, he may have been a member of the choir of twenty-five gentlemen who

[1] Misc. Bk., T. R., No. 216, at the Record Office.

accompanied the Court in the summer of 1520 to Guisnes for the Field of the Cloth of Gold.

Of these singing men we know that one, Thomas Farthing, died in December 1520. He had been in receipt of an annuity of ten marks from the manors of Torpull and Makesey in Northamptonshire, and this very annuity was transferred on February 12, 1520, to John Heywood "in consideracione boni et fidelis servicii quod serviens noster Johes Haywode," etc.[1] Faithful service generally implies long service.[2]

There is after this unfortunately a break in the King's Quarterly Accounts until Michaelmas 1526, when the item appears:

To John Heywood Pleyar of the virginals . . . £6 13. 4.

The virginal, like the spinet, the clavichord, and the harpsichord, was the predecessor of the piano. It was perhaps an instrument used originally for hymns to the Virgin. We are told that Queen Elizabeth "exercised herself dailie in plaieing at the recorders, flute, virginals, in setting of songs and making of ballads." In an old inventory is an item of "two fair pair of new long Virginalls made harp fashion of Cipres with keys of ivory." Princess Mary played the virginal. Her annual expenses for tuition were heavy. Edward VI had three players whom Mary retained when she came to the throne.

I cannot refrain here from quoting Collier,[3] who wrote in 1831, "we have a detailed and accurate account of the whole domestic establishment of Henry VIII in the seventeenth year of his reign (i.e. 1525–6). I have a contemporary manuscript in my possession endorsed 'a Booke of Wages paide monethly, quarterly and half-yerly by the King, 17 Henry

[1] Privy Seal Warr., No. 499.

[2] Cf. Henry VIII papers. Patent Rolls, February 1521, "Grant to John Heywood of an annuity of 10 marks of the manors of Makesey and Torpull, Northampton vice Thomas Farthing."

[3] J. Payne Collier, *Annals of the Stage*, 1831, vol. 1, p. 94.

VIII.' Here we find the names and salaries of every person connected with the household from the highest to the lowest, but on what occasion it was made out does not anywhere appear.

12 Trumpettes wages in 16d a daye	24*l.*
3 other Trumpettes wages in 8d a daye	40s.
Giles Lewter with the Princess	40s.
Arthur Dewer, Lewter	10s. 4d.
Peter Welder, Lewter	31s.
John Severnake a rebike	40s.
Balthazar a taberet	31s.
William More Harper	10/4d.
Hause Hoffenet Vial	31/4d.
Jaques Phipher	31/–
A Sagbut	55/6
For borde wages of the children of the Chapel to Maister Crane	26/8
Lord of Mysrule	30/–
John Heywood pleyar of the virginals	£6. 13. 4."

This record, I think, gives one an idea of Heywood's professional position at Henry's Court and it seems likely that he was actively employed there as a singer and a player till November 8, 1528, when he was granted an "Annuell Pension" of £10 a year for life. Note of this payment appears in the surviving *Bokes of Paymentes*—there are some gaps—from 1528 to 1551.

What exactly was his social position at Court, especially between 1519 and 1528, it is not easy to determine. He said of himself:

> Longe have I been a *singinge man*
> And sondree partes often I have songe
> Yet one part since I first began
> I cold or can sing olde or younge
> The meane I meane which parte showeth well
> Above all partes most to excell.[1]

C. W. Wallace, who is often inclined to dogmatize on

---

[1] Collier, i, 73 *n.* Cotton MS., Vesp. A.xxv.

slight premisses, says of him that he was a *Court entertainer*; that is to say, not much else, with the status of an actor or a pierrot in Victorian society.

Bishop Bale in 1548 describes him as "Orpheus alter," which can only refer to his singing voice, and says that he was "instrumentorum studiosus musicus et poeta. Magnam habebat in sua lingua gratiam. Hujus ab amplo ac sollerti ingenio plura exierunt lectoribus non injucunda." This some have regarded as faint praise and not indicative of a scholar. But a man is not called *Orpheus* for nothing.

Also, Antony à Wood says "he was in much esteem with King Henry VIII for the mirth and quickness of his conceits and though he had little learning in him; yet he was by that King well rewarded." King Henry's high esteem either of a musician or a man cannot go for nothing.

Johannes Pitseus in *De Rebus Anglicis*, 1619, adds that he was "Valde ingeniosus musices quam vocalis quam instrumentalis peritus elegans in Poesi et plus quam credi potest in familiari colloquio lepidus atque facetus. In salibus mire acutus."

This says much for what Horace would call his *communis sensus*; not so much "common sense" as social sense, ability to move easily in all circles, professional, courtly, or scholarly.

His social position, therefore, was probably higher than has been generally supposed. He was something more than the Court jester, Will Summers—"Sot Somer"—on whom he pours all the vials of scorn twice in *Wytty and Wyttles*; and of whom Matthew Sutcliffe writes:

> But if Will Summers had written this discourse
> He could never have spoken more foolishly nor impertinently.
> *Answer to Parsons*, 1604

At the same time his status cannot have been very high, for he was for some time receiving not much more than "a gardyner."

It is most probable he had no specified position at Court but was only a licensed favourite, or a personal attendant, with a nominal role like that of *dapifer camerae* or sewer, one who was expected to be a literary and musical handyman and on occasion to be the actor-manager at the Court.

Writing of Heywood's position in the reign of Edward VI, George Puttenham[1] says "there came to be in reputation for the same faculties [in "vulgar makings"] John Heywood the epigrammatist who for the myrth and quickness of his conceits more than for any good learning was in him came to be well benefitted by the King."

But in William Camden's *Remains,* 1870, are related anecdotes which, perhaps, best illustrate his status, and incidentally the watery kind of humour that went down well in those days.

"When Queen Mary told Heywood that the priests must forgo their wives he merrily answered: 'Your grace must allow them lemans, for the clergy cannot live without sauce.'

"Again he being asked of the said Queen Mary what wind blew him to Court, answered: 'Two, firstly the one to see your Majesty.' 'We thank you for that,' said Queen Mary, 'but I pray you, what is the other?' 'That your Grace,' said he, 'might see me.'

"Again when he saw one riding that bare a wanton behind him, he said, 'In good faith, sir, I should say your horse were overladen, if I did not perceive that the lady you carry is very light.' "

Puttenham tells another grand watery joke from which modern students of psychology will draw their own conclusions.

"The like happened at the Duke of Northumberland's board when merry John Heywood *was allowed to sit at the table's end.* The Duke had a very noble and honorable mynde always to pay his debts well and when he lacked money

[1] In the *Arte of English Poesie,* 1890.

would not stick to sell the greatest part of his plate. So had he done few days before. Heywood being loth to call for drinks so oft as he was dry, turned his eye toward the cupboard and sayd: 'I find great misse of your graces standing cups.' The Duke, thinking he had spoken it of some knowledge that his plate was lately sold, said somewhat sharply, 'Why, sir, will not these cuppes serve as good a man as your selfe?' Heywood readily replied: 'Yes, if it please your Grace, but I would have one of them stand still at myne elbow full of drinke that I might not be driven to trouble your men so often as to call for it.' This pleasant and speedy revers of the former wordes holpe all the matter again. Whereupon the Duke became very pleasaunt and drank a bolle of wine to Heywood and bid a cup should always be standing by him."

Of his status Dr. J. S. Farmer wrote it was "superior and more assured than is generally supposed." But to me Heywood was in the genealogy of the jesters and the minstrels, and though he was superior to his pedigree it seems impossible to grant him a very high caste, though Sir Thomas More was his Maecenas; though he and his wife later were of sufficient standing and close enough intimates of the Mores to be specially informed of the comment of the Emperor Charles on Sir Thomas's execution; and though the Princesses Mary and Elizabeth were also his patrons and frequently gave him gratuities of thirty shillings.

I should say that he was a favourite with Henry VIII mainly as a musician with a good voice and a broad sense of humour. But I think it not unlikely that as his genius and versatility began to flower in his proverbs, epigrams, poems, and plays, his social position improved gradually from that of a Court servant to that of a gentleman, who had achieved a final position by his mature talents and their financial success.

It is likely that after 1528, when he would be just over thirty, he began his serious literary work and that it was this which distracted him from the Court.

There is no need to construe the grant of a pension in 1528 as a sentence of dismissal and as a loss of the royal favour. It may be taken, rather, as an indication that he had outgrown his original station. Indeed, the Town Clerk's Records at the Guildhall show that even in 1523 on the request of the King he had been admitted at a Common Council to the Freedom of the City. Again in 1529 in the same records we are told that John Heywood, "oon of the kynges seruauntes," was admitted as a "comen mesurer or meter of linnen clothes into the mistery of mercers." Again in the State Papers of Henry VII, 1532–3, among those signalized by a new year gift from the King is recorded:

Heywood, Item a gilte cuppe with a couer weing XXIII oz.

He did not receive another royal favour till November 21, 1540, when he was restored the lease of the manor of "Brook-hall" ("Brokehall"), near Tiptree, in Essex, for twenty-one years at a rent of £14 2s. 6d.[1] Also, at some date unknown, the King may have rewarded him with another manor, viz. at Haydon in Essex, the owner of which had become the victim of attainder. But the facts of this are not known yet.

Therefore it seems likely that though in receipt of his pension he gradually faded out of the Court picture, and became a *dapifer camerae* or honorary sewer of the chamber to Henry VIII, Edward VI, and Mary: a sewer being the unpromising title of an official who originally had the doubtful privilege of discovering[2] whether the royal fare were poisoned or only badly cooked.

We have now come to the most important period of Heywood's life, from 1528, when his first period of Court

---

[1] He had had the lease before the Dissolution of the Monasteries from the Abbey of St. Osyths. When the abbey was dissolved Cromwell seized the manor, but on Cromwell's execution Heywood reclaimed it and got it at an increased rent and on a shorter lease.

[2] Essayer and Essuyer.

activity ended, till 1552, when his second period under
Edward VI and Mary began. It was a troublous time. The
garish ostentation of the Field of the Cloth of Gold had
yielded to the melancholy materialism of divorce. Wolsey had
fallen, and the reign of a dictator had begun. Utopia and the
Platonic socialism or Christian Humanism, dear to More and
John Rastell, were more remote than ever. Cranmer was
vacillating and unorthodox and had at last decreed the King's
marriage void.

✳ It was at this time (particularly 1533) that the younger
Rastell began to print some of the six plays which are now
assigned without doubt to Heywood, viz.:

    1. *Wytty and Wyttles.*
    2. *The Play of Loue.*
    3. *The Wether.*
    4. *The Pardoner and the Frere.*
    5. *The Foure P.P.*
    6. *Johan Johan.*[1]

It was at this time also (perhaps 1528) that Heywood began
his bitter and tedious allegory of *The Spider and the Flie*, in
which he perhaps was thinking of Cranmer as the Spider and
John Rastell as "the imprisoned flie," condemned to prison
as a Natural Thinker and an opponent of tithes.

When one considers the public attitude to players and
playwrights in later times it is surprising to see the place that
Heywood took in the world of the day.

He was intimate with Sir Thomas More, with whom he had
common intellectual, religious, and marital interests, as we
have seen, and by whom he may have been sent to Oxford.

More perhaps introduced him to the Court. It is very

---

[1] Many have also assigned *Gentylnes and Nobylyte* to Heywood. But
Dr. Reed, by a citation of parallel passages from the *Pastime of the
People*, *The Boke of Purgatory*, and *The Four Elements*, shows it to be
without doubt the work of John Rastell.

plausible that he inspired part of Heywood's work and that Heywood saw, for instance, a book like *Utopia* in the making in 1515. His big allegory of *The Spider and the Flie*, which I shall consider later, may have been initiated or inspired by his friend himself.

It is not unlikely that More and More's circle brought Heywood also into touch with the leading musicians and playwrights of the day; so that he came to be esteemed the authority at royal plays and pageants.

For instance, in Thomas Cromwell's Book of Accounts[1] is an item for February 21, 1539:

> Payed to the Paynter that made all the hobby horses and the other things ther belonging £33. 17. 6. Heywoode The same daye paied to him for his coste & other necessaries layed out £6. 10. 5.

This has probably to do with a "maske" *King Arthur's Knights*, written perhaps by Heywood and produced within a few months of the Chancellor's execution in 1540.

There can be no doubt that More introduced him to that group of whom he, Colet, and Erasmus were the chief, who eagerly took up the renaissance of learning, and restudied the New Testament in the original.

Here we must emphasize the uncompromising Catholicism of Heywood. Some have gone so far as to deny him the authorship of any of the "Heywood" plays which make an attack on the Church. But that is to ignore the spirit of More and Heywood. Heywood saw abuses in the Church not less than Chaucer, Langland, and Hoccleve, from all of whom he borrowed. He was ready for changes. But like the Oxford Reformers he did not support in any way the Lutheran doctrine, against which Henry VIII had written his book. More met his death in 1535 only because he would not consent to what must have seemed to some a not very fundamental breach with Catholicism. From More one can know his friend.

[1] R. O. Excheq. Misc. T. R. Misc., Bk. 256.

Pitseus comments on the piety of Heywood (*vir pius*) and Wood states that after Queen Mary's decease "he left the nation for religion's sake and settled at Mechlin in Brabant. Which is a wonder to some who will allow no religion in poets that this should above all of his profession be a voluntary exile for it." We shall see later that both he and his sons surrendered considerable wealth in England for their religion's sake, and occupied a remarkable position among the Jesuits in the Low Countries.

In 1534 the political break between England and Rome had been authorized by the Act of Supremacy. Cranmer was the Primate and a court under his presidency declared that Henry's marriage with Catharine (of whom only one child, the Princess Mary, survived) was "null and void." This widened the breach with Rome. The King had declared that he was Head of the Church, had repudiated the Pope's authority, and had dissolved the monasteries. At the same time in 1539 the Six Articles Statute was passed, strongly affirming Catholic doctrines and declaring that those who denied the doctrine of Transubstantiation should be burnt as heretics. Bishop Fisher of Rochester and Sir Thomas More declined to accept part of the new policy and met their fate in 1535.

It was the Act of Supremacy and not the Six Articles which disturbed them. These Six Articles, because of their strict provisions, were nicknamed "the whip with six strings." In addition to enforcing the dogma of Transubstantiation they enjoined celibacy on the priests and inculcated the value of private masses and auricular confession. In fact they were helpful in every way to the cause of orthodox Catholicism.

Yet though the tenor of his life shows that he was an orthodox Catholic and that there could have been nothing in the Six Articles Statute that could cause him qualms, there is almost contemporary evidence that Heywood's life was in danger through religion.

J. Harington in his *Metamorphosis of Ajax* exclaims in 1596: "What thynke you by Haywode that scaped hanging with hys mirth, the king being graciously, as I think, persuaded that a man that wrot so pleasant and harmless verses could not have a harmful conceit against his proceedings; and so by the honest notion of a gentleman of his chamber saved him from the jerk of the six stringed whip. This Haywood for his Proverbs and Epigrams is not yet put down by any of our country though one doth indeed come near him that graces him the more in saying he puts him down."

There therefore appears to be a confusion in Harington's mind between the Six Articles Statute and the Act of Supremacy. The Six Articles of 1539 would not worry the confirmed Catholics who went to the other extreme and martyred themselves for the Act of Supremacy of 1534.

This view of Heywood appears to be confirmed in the Wriothesley Chronicles, which read "The sixth day of July (1544) Hayward recanted his treason at Pawles Crosse which had been afore condempned to death and brought to be layd on the hardell for denying the Supremacy of the kings Majestie against the Bishop of Rome," and again in John Foxe's *Actes and Monuments*, of 1563: "The same yere also followed the recantatyon of John Heywoode who although he was tached for treason for denying the kinges supremacye yet usinge the clemency of the king upon his better reformation and amendment made an open and solempne recantatyon in the face of all people abandoning and renouncing the Pope's thrasonicall supremacy and confessinge the kinge chief supreame head and governour of the Church of England, all soveraine autoritye and jurisdiction beinge excluded." "The tenor and effect" of his "recantatyon" is then given:

The Recantation of John Heywood.

I am come hether at this time good people willingly and of mine oune desirous sute. . . . I do utterly and with al my hart recant and revoke

al mine aforesaid and erroneous and traiterous opinione. The bishop of
Rome has [authority] only within the precincts of his own diocese and
the king is the supreme head of the church of England.[1]

But it is clear at any rate that the years from 1540, after
he had received from the King the manor of Brokehall, to
July 6, 1544, when he recanted, were precarious for Heywood.
It seems likely that he was implicated in the plot of the ultra-
Catholics against Cranmer, who was supported by Henry VIII,
and that he barely escaped. Power had fallen into the hands
of Norfolk and the Catholics and a plot was afoot against
Cranmer, who was too progressive or too elastic. Heywood
was probably implicated in this plot against a cleric whom
Henry would not abandon; and he was condemned to forfeit
his life and his property.

In the *Interrogatories* drawn up by Cranmer against John
Parkehurst in 1543 the name of "Mr. Moore and all the friends
of Sir Thomas More, including 'Haywode' are mentioned."[2]

Similarly, when on April 24, 1544, John More, son of Sir
Thomas, was "pardoned by all treasonable words with the
detestable traitors," the traitors' names included John
Heywood's.

On July 20, 1544, a general pardon dated at Westminster
was granted to John Heywode, late of London, alias of North
Mimmes, Herts, and his property was restored,[3] and we are
glad to find this pious playwright in receipt of his royal
pension in 1545. Perhaps he was, on occasion, too orthodox
a Catholic for Henry VIII. "Liberos suos in timore Dei solli-
cite educavit et in bonis litteris atque in fide Catholica optime

---

[1] Memorandum quod supra scripta assertio sive recantatio fuit facta
et publice emissa per prenominatum Johannem Heiwood die dominico,
sexto viz die Julii. An millesimo quingentesimo quadragesimo quarto
apud crucem paulinam.

[2] "What communication had you by word or writing with Mr.
Roper Balthasar the Surgeon Mr. Moore, Haywode . . . ?"

[3] Patent Rolls 1544 pro Johe Heywode de Pardonacione.

institui fecit. . . . Duos filios habuit societatis Jesu pres-
byteros."

In 1547 came quieter times; it may be that he had learnt
his lesson and that he engrossed himself with his young family.
For probably about 1523 he had married John Rastell's
daughter Joan.[1] So he lived out the rest of the reign of Henry
peaceably.

The boy King, Puttenham tells us, appreciated his wit
too, and appointed him *dapifer camerae*, and granted him in
1552 a pension of £40 in place of the old pension of £10. And
no doubt Heywood took a large part in the numerous pageants
which were devised to cheer the boy's drooping spirits.[2]

I have encountered somewhere in the Losely manuscript
of the period a reference to a revel when the Revels Officer
prepared apparel for the twelve children of the Chapel[3] in a
play "that Haywode mad"; and again on February 12, 1553,
"A play of the state of Ierland and another of children sett
owte by Mr. Haywood and dyvers oth. players and pastymes
appareled furnyshed and wrought upon within the Office of
the Revels"; and again on April 1, 1553, "Dew unto John
roberttes lynnen draper ffor XXIII elles bockrom at XII's the
elle for the making of XII cotes for the boyes in Heywoode's
play."

When Mary "came to the thrown," says Wood, "Heywood
was much valued by her and often had the honour to wait
on her and exercise his fancy before her: which he did even
to the time that she lay languishing on her death bed."

---

[1] She died about 1573.

[2] "He was well benefitted by the King for the myrth & quickness
of his conceits." George Puttenham, *Of poets and poesie*, i, XXXI.

[3] It is not always clear who "the children" were; whether they were
the children of the Royal Chapel or the children of St. Paul's School,
which was famous for its troupe. Cf. the long reference in *Hamlet* to
the "eyrie of children," "little eyases," etc., and Ben Jonson's admiring
words on the premature death of Salathiel Pavey, "who played old men
so duly."

This was not surprising from a good Catholic for at a time, 1533–4, when Princess Mary was under a cloud of disgrace, as illegitimate and barred from the succession on account of the nullity of her mother's marriage with Henry, and with scarcely a friend in the world, Heywood had written of her *The Description of a Most Noble Lady*:

> The vertue of her lookes
> Excells the precious stone;
> Yee need none other bookes
> To reede or looke upon
>
> In each of her two uyes
> Ther smiles a naked boye
> It would you all suffice
> Too see those lampes of joye
>
> I think nature hath lost her moulde
> When shee her forme dyd take
> Or ells I doubt it nature coulde
> So fair a creature make.

In her Privy Purse expenses for January 1536 there is an item: "Itm gevn to Heywood sunte for bringing of my Ladys grace regalles from London to Grenewich xxd." This has led to the belief that Heywood was a musical tutor to Mary when she was a princess.

Times were now more secure for the playwright and he could indulge his religious fancy. It was about this time that he concluded his allegory *The Spider and the Flie*, of which Mary was perhaps "the heroine" in its final complimentary form, but which he dared not to publish till she was crowned.[1]

---

[1] John Stow in his *Annales*, 1617 (p. 239), records that when Queen Mary at her coronation rode through the City attended by the Lady Elizabeth and the Lady Anne of Cleves, amongst many pageants presented to her "in Paul's Churchyard against the schools, one Mr. Heywood sate in a pageant under a vine and made to her an oration in Latin and English."

Heywood was very prosperous under his latest royal protector. His pension was raised to £50 in 1555; and it may have been during this reign that he was granted the reversion of land in Romney Marsh. I cannot trace the date of the grant of this property, to which reference is made in Heywood's letter to Lord Burghley in 1575 and in the "Fugitive" Inquisition held in the fourteenth year of Elizabeth's reign.

When Mary married Philip of Spain, Heywood celebrated the event in "A Balade specifienge partly the maner partly the matter, in the most excellent meetyng and lyke mariage betwene our sovereigne Lord and our soveraigne Lady, the Kynges and Quenes Highnes":[1]

> So meete a matche in parentage
> So meete a matche in dignite
> So meete a matche in patronage
> So meete a match in benignite
> So matcht from all malignite
> As thanks to God gyven for the same
> Seelde hathe been seene: thus sayeth the fame.
>
> This meete-met matche at first meeting
> In theyr aproche togither neere
> Loulie lovelie lyveli gretting
> In eche to other did so appere
> That lookers on al must graunt cleere
> Theire usage of suche humayne reache
> As all might lerne but none coulde teache.

This is artificial, fulsome, and typical of our hero. But from many references it is clear that he was popular with Mary, both when she was Princess and when Queen; and that he could make even the iron muscles of her face relax. His strange blend of religion, humour, good sense, and patriotism was the secret of his success with her. He helped to amuse her even on her deathbed, so the story goes.

[1] Pende by John Heywood and imprinted at London by Wyllyam Ryddell.

In his epigram "On Rebellion" he declares his fealty to her—the fealty which, despite his religious fits, he had to all the Tudors:

> Being true to God, Queen, Country, and Crown.

Similarly he says:

> Wilt thou be taken for a true English man?
> Yea? Be true to God, thy Queen and Country than.
> Stand fast by thy Country whoever would win it.

And in the "Conclusion" of the long allegory of *The Spider and the Flie*, which he could not resume safely till Mary's accession and which he then remodelled into a complimentary poem, he writes in this vein:

> To the maid, as spiders and flies to that maid,
> Let our banners of obedience be displayed,
> Of love, the badge of rejoicing, the right root,
> And of our wealth the right and full boot.
> Love we her, and obey we her, as we ought,
> And also our sovereign Lord Philip, to her brought
> By God, as God brought her to us. Which twain
> Conjoined one in matrimonial train,
> But one also in authority regal.
> These two thus made one, both one here we call;
> Which two thus one, rejoice we every one.

On November 10, 1558, his pension of £50 was annulled at his own wish when she granted him the lease of the manor of Bolmer.[1]

When his royal friend and patron died times were changing. He was getting old, the only thing that had not changed was his religion. So "After the Queen's decease," says Wood, "he left the Nation for religion sake." He did not leave at once.

---

[1] Bulmer in Yorkshire, of which the Duke of Leeds is now Lord of the Manor. State Papers, "Domestic," xiv, 8, November 10, 1558. "Grant of a lease for forty years to John Heywood of the Manor of Bolmer in Yorkshire at the rent of £30 for his life."

THE
UNIVERSITY OF WINNIPEG
PORTAGE & BALMORAL
WINNIPEG 2. MAN.   CANADA

For we read in Henry Machyn's *Diary*, 1559, that on August 5, 1559, when the Queen's Grace "removyed from Eltham into Nonshyche," there was a great "soper, bankett and maske" and "a playe of ye chylderyn of Powlls," at which Heywood assisted.

Further, it has been argued firstly that as Jasper Heywood dedicated his work to the Chancellor of Oxford in 1559; and secondly that as in Thomas Powell's 1562 edition of the *Epigrammes*,[1] reads: "Thanks to God and good people Powles goeth up well," which may be taken as an allusion of the rebuilding by public subscription of St. Paul's, struck by lightning and partially destroyed on June 4, 1561—the Heywood family was still in England in 1561.

Wood says that he died in 1565. But W. Bang[2] quotes the will of William Rastell, signed and dated 1565, bequeathing a ring to John Heywood.[3] And from a book printed in 1570 by John Day, called *Recantation of the Famous Pasquin of Rome*, it is clear that he was alive in 1570.

The time of Heywood's death was not yet. He was to end his days in exile some years later.

Queen Elizabeth's Religious Settlement[4] drove Heywood and his circle into voluntary exile. The moderate Parker was now the Primate and the Act of Uniformity was being enforced. Furthermore Rome had categorically prohibited all true Catholics from appearing at public worship in England.

Heywood left England for ever on July 20, 1564, leaving his property in the care of his son-in-law, John Donne.

Several Commissions followed the Catholic plots against

---

[1] No. 62 "of a sixt hundred of Epigrammes newly invented and made by John Heywood."

[2] In *Acta Anglo-Louaniensia*, 1907.

[3] "Item do et lego Domino Johanni Heywood patri dicti Elizei annulum aureum meum."

[4] The Articles of Religion in 1563 and the Act of Uniformity in 1554.

Elizabeth, of which four are extant, including the Hertford-shire Commission,[1] which ran:

(1) That the said John Heywood and his son, English subjects, on July 20, 1564, contemptuously departed and fled without license into parts across the sea in Flanders and Brabant under the obedience of Philip and Spain and that, in spite of a proclamation calling upon them to return they had refused to do so.

(2) That John Heywood owned a tenement of forty acres, called Butlers held by customary tenure of the Lord of the Manor of North Mymmes, and a second tenement called Iveries which he leased of the same Lord of the Manor November 2, 1540.

(3) That Ellis Heywood also had a property in North Mymmes called Hawkeshall which he had by the gift of Mr. Rastell.

(4) That the rent of these tenements had been collected for John and Ellis by John Donne, ironmonger, up to the Lady Day 1571, and after that by Elizabeth Marvin, widow daughter of John Heywood.

(5) That Joan, wife of John Heywood, died before the holding of the Inquest in 1574.

The rest of the life of Heywood is known to us from several unexpected sources. We are left with an impression of great prosperity in England abandoned for conscience' sake, and of self-sacrifice. Writing from Louvain in 1571 Nicolaus Sanderus[2] among "viri nobiles ob fidem Catholicam in exilio degentes" mentioned John Heywood. He excuses himself for giving the bare names of the others—"Quos ob fidem Catholicam aut carcerem aut exilium passos esse aut a locupletissimis testibus accepi, aut ipsi cognovi."

He mentions as dead at Louvain, Heywood's brother-in-law William Rastell, "civilium et criminalium causarum judex," "sub Edwardo sexto exulans," "ac iterum sub Elizabetha in exilium sponte redeuns."

Again, about 1583, Io Aquepontanus[3] in *Index Personarum*, "quae ad nostram notitiam pervenerunt quae propter fidem Catholicam passae sunt exilium sub Elizabetha Regina," men-

---

[1] Quoted by Dr. A. W. Reed.
[2] In *De Visibili Monarchia Ecclesiae*.   [3] John Bridgwater.

tioned "Gaspar Haywode Nobilis, Sacerdos, Theologiae Doctor."

In *Concertatio Ecclesiae* he shows that John Heywood in 1578 was known as an octogenarian, and as a benefactor of the Society of Jesus.

In *L'Histoire de la Compagnie de Jésus à Anvers*, Father Droueshout, s.j., shows that in 1573 Ellis Heywood came from England to Antwerp to discuss matters with the magistrate of the city where his knowledge of several languages was useful; and that his father was then living at Malines, come from England, "persécuté pour la foi." "Il s'y était rétabli."

The son went to comfort his father. But this disturbed the son's work, so Father Mercurian, "Général de la Compagnie, autorisa les Pères de la Résidence d'Anvers à admettre au Collège avec logement et tables séparés ce digne vieillard. Cette admission se fit 1576."

When religious troubles recurred at Antwerp in 1578 the Jesuits decided to send to Cologne "quelques uns des nôtres qui auraient plus de difficulté à se sauver par la fuite." "Nous éloignions d'abord Jean Haywodus vieillard octogénaire avec un de nos religieux pour l'accompagner et le conduire jusqu'à cette ville."

But the party with old Heywood was stopped at the gate of the town and their religious opponents compelled them to return to Antwerp. This was in April.

Later, as the Jesuits declined to swear what they regarded as a criminal oath[1] the college at Antwerp was broken into and sacked and all the Fathers made prisoners, including, I suppose, John and Ellis Heywood.

They were to be sent by water to Malines. But the Prince of Orange sent a courier to Malines ordering the magistrates to keep the prisoners outside the gates, and secretly despatched

[1] To acknowledge the Pacification of Ghent and to fight against the Spaniards.

sixty horsemen to await them and kill them there. But the prisoners, while on the water, addressed themselves to the Commandant, who sent to the Commandant at Lierre, asking him to bring over to Malines an escort for the prisoners and to send a courier to Louvain to Don Juan, the Spanish commander, asking him to do the same and meet the Fathers midway between Malines and Louvain.

The prisoners reached Malines. Here they were refused admission and narrowly escaped death. Fortunately, at half-past six in the evening the escort arrived from Lierre, and, later, "tous entrent triomphalement à Louvain le xxvi Mai 1578."

Heywood was one of the benefactors of the Order and Wood tells us that he lived on till 1585 at Malines, which was to be his burial ground; leaving behind him several children, to whom he had given a liberal education, among whom were Ellis and Jasper, the former Bachelor of Civil Law and Fellow of All Souls in 1548, and the latter a Master of Arts, and "both afterwards noted Jesuits."

Ellis travelled in France and Italy under the patronage of Cardinal Pole and wrote *Il Moro*, 1556, dedicated to the Cardinal.

Jasper had soon left Oxford, where he had been probationer Fellow at Merton, to become a Jesuit. He wrote various poems and "devises" and translations. His translations in a rugged verse of Seneca's *Troas*, *Thyestes*, and *Hercules Furens* in 1559, 1560, and 1561 were not without some distinction. Later on he appears to have become very prosperous, with the mien of a baron rather than a priest. He travelled much on the Continent, leaving his father to the custody of Ellis, the most devoted of sons, who died on October 2, 1578.

John Heywood was now at Malines alone. On April 18, 1575, he had written to Lord Burghley the letter with which I began this chapter. From its contents it could only be his:

'Right honorable and my verie good Lord: I understand of late what a good earnest sewtor it hath pleased my good honorable Ladie your good wiffe to be for me, nowe in my poore old age when my friendes are in a manner all dead and manie of them utterlie forsaken me and my wholle lyvying detayned from me and the chieffest part of it which was a lease for yeares in Romney Marshe begged and bought away utterlie from me; And neither of that nor of the rest not one pennye of it paid or sent hither unto me for my maintenance for these twoo yeares and a half: And nowe it pleaseth your good Lordship as I heare to comaund my sonne Doonne to send me over the arrerages which hath bein deteyned from me. I beseche god reward and blesse the quenes hignes and your good honor for it as also my good ladie who hath ever bene my good ladie and nowe my special good Ladie And though Beggars may not be chusers yet they may be cravers I will moost humblie therefore crave of the quenes Magestie and desyr moost humblie your honour and my good Ladie to be sewtors for me to her magestie that I maye enjoye the rest of my poore lyving here quietlie by her highnes lycence and pattent to me and my assygnes duryng my liffe which can not be by all lykeliehoode aboue twoo or three yeares being nowe LXXVIII years of age. And I will God willing your honor shall never heare anie otherwise of me than becometh a poore honest quyett old man but will spend my tyme that I have to lyve in prayer and in loking to my last ende which cannot be longe seing my hearing begynneth to fayle me and my myrth decayeth with age and my bodie is weake. . . . From mechlyne where I have bein sore sacked and spoyled of a goode part of that littill that I had both by spanyards and Germayns soldiars which hath made my purse bare. And therefore good my Lord help to comfort it agayne This XVIII of Aprell 1.5.7.5.

Your honors most hombyll orator

as he ys greatly bownden

JHON HEYWOOD[1]

---

[1] The Egerton Papers (1840, p. 63) contain a list of Roman Catholic fugitives dated January 29, 1576, "when probably their names were certified into the exchequer as absent from the Kingdom" contrary to the statute of 1571. Among them "John Heywood, Gent, holding land in Kent and resident at Louvain" is mentioned as "of Kent." This is probably the dramatist, but it is not clear if he is on a list of *living* fugitives. It is possible that when the return was completed Heywood was dead and that no account of his death had been received in England. The same list is found elsewhere.

He wrote a second letter in the same tenor, showing that there was still a glint of fire in the old furnace, to Lord Burghley in September 1575, from which we are glad to find that his first letter had been received sympathetically at Court and that he had received what we hope was an instalment, viz. of £50 of the "arrerages" upon his Kent estate.

In 1587 Thomas Newton in his Epilogue speaks of the old man with the mad merry wit (mentioning his name) as:

> dead and gone and shrined in tombs of clay
> Now as wee may a lyon soone discerne even by his pawe
> So by this works we quickly a judgement certain drawe
> What kind of man the author was and what a pleasant vaine
> Of fancy's forge and modest mirth lay lodged in his braine.
> Let him therefore that gathered first these Proverbs fine and brave
> With roundly couched Epigrammes a friendly censure have
> That others may of ashes his bee raised like paines to take
> In hope to worke their countries weale and so an ende I make.

Indeed it is probable that the old man did not long survive the deaths of his son Ellis and of his life-long friend William Roper, who died in 1578. His son Jasper survived till 1597–8 and his daughter Elizabeth, mother of the poet and preacher John Donne, Dean of St. Paul's, lived well into the next century.

Pitseus has embalmed the old man's last joke. He was dying and it was his last chance: "Cum sua peccata praeterita multum deploraret et bonus quidam sacerdos illud solum responderet et identidem repeteret 'carnem esse fragilem'; retulit ille 'ne tu Deum arguere videris, quod me non fecerit piscem,' " which may be translated roughly: "When he was regretting his past sins and the good priest only said and kept on saying, 'The flesh is weak,' he retorted 'You seem to be blaming God for not making me a fish.' "

*   *   *   *   *

Enough has been said to indicate the significance of this man and what has not been said is implied in his work, some of which follows.

He was a self-made man of humble origin. He had that nimbleness of genius which, like Shakespeare's, rose superior to school and university. Human life was his target and he took up his shaft unhampered by technique and tradition. His ready wit, his power of observation, his facile self-expression, his self-confidence, his courage, found him favour with all and not least with the intelligentsia of the country and of the Court.

He was a sound patriot, and if his religious principles might carry him on occasion too far for his personal safety and comfort, they were only to his credit. And no doubt that was the view that Henry took of it in the end.

Heywood gave pleasure wherever he went by his bright conversation, by his forthright good nature, by his singing, by his instrumental music, and by his plays.

The genealogy of these plays may begin in the contemporary French farces and a situation in one of Heywood's plays is clearly plagiarized. But the value of origins is always exaggerated.

The truth is that Heywood's dramatic work taken at its climax with *Johan* or *The Foure P.P.* is an entire novelty. These plays are not Miracle plays and with two exceptions they are not Morality plays. Even in the plays which most correspond with the Morality the characters are not abstractions but human beings. Heywood drove the Church, the Priest, and the Bible off the stage. He restored the straightforward native humour of Chaucer, including that coarse humour which is one of the sincerest and most laughable things in life. He then went on to present a familiar domestic scene which is the basis of comedy to-day. He must be accorded a high place in the annals of the English stage.

ANALYSIS

I shall now give an analysis of the six undoubted plays of John Heywood, viz. *Wytty and Wyttles, Loue, The Wether, The Pardoner and the Frere, The Foure P.P., Johan Johan*; and of Heywood's other undoubted works, *A Dialogue, The Epigrammes, The Spider and the Flie.*

In this analysis I have given the source of the text; I have given the argument or the outline in brief; I have examined all the internal evidence.

I particularly commend my readers to study some at least of the work of John Heywood in its entirety. It has an interest *per se.* But it has a greater interest in its portrayal of the Elizabethan mentality and of what an Elizabethan audience could endure and perhaps could endure with pleasure.

I

WYTTY AND WYTTLES

THIS play is complete but for the title and part of the introduction. The original manuscript, which in spite of a few
corrections and erasures may be a fair copy, is in the British
Museum. It was edited for the Percy Society by F. W. Fair-
holt. The text which I give is, I believe, slightly more correct,
though the document is nowhere a sight for tired eyes. It is
never easy to be sure of the spelling—particularly of the
final *e*'s.

The manuscript unquestionably belongs to the sixteenth
century; it has been assigned by experts without query to the
reign of Henry VIII. This is confirmed by the comparative
uncouthness of its spelling, by its references to Will Summers[1]
Henry's jester, and by the three crude staves about the King
with which it concludes.

It is imperfect, but very little, except the title and the
introduction, has been lost. It concludes with an autograph:
"Amen qd. John Heywod."

We are therefore lucky in beginning a criticism of Heywood's work by an examination of a work which undoubtedly
must be attributed to him.

Wytty and Wyttles is an interlude rather than a play.
This form of entertainment was often, as here, a dialogue
which took place in public—a discussion, debate, or exercise

---

[1] Mayster Somer the Kyngys gracys foole.
"A gentle delicate fool with a kind heart, a great favourite with
Henry VIII, who adopted an outward folly."
(Robert Armin: *Nest of Ninnies*, 1608.)

In *The Arte of Rhetorique* in 1553 Wilson refers to his witty confusion
of frauditors with auditors.

in dialectic, in which each point or quibble was closely followed. One wonders how an entertainment of this kind could ever have been popular; though I think no significance need be attached to the fact that it only survives in manuscript. It is certainly very dull; I venture to say the dullest literary effort in the world, though it has a close rival in *The Play of Loue.*

But it probably was not dull at the time of its composition. It was a favourite exercise at the universities to indulge discussions in which, in the interest of dialectic and as a sort of mental gymnastic, one party took up an outrageous standpoint, as *advocatus diaboli,* from which another tried to dislodge him.

To anyone who is willing to project himself into the sixteenth century and conjure up the scene, the shrewd lunges and ripostes, the points complacently scored, with much inward smugness by the author, together with the author's laboured tricks of style, the convenient *deus ex machina* when the argument is becoming too intricate, and the three naïve staves of music at the end extravagantly lauding His Majesty's wit, staves which in his absence are "voyd"—the reading of the play will not be ungrateful.

But the reader must be a student of humanity and be interested in the evolution of English humour, which, for the moment, owing to the dour influence of the Church, had lapsed from the days of Chaucer.

This interlude must be regarded as a good specimen of the courtly amusement of the Tudor age. It is a dramatic form of the medieval "Debat, Strif or Estrif."

Heywood was not the only one to see that if these poetic controversies were to be acted publicly some farcical element of disorder must be introduced.

Furthermore, it must be studied for the light it throws upon the "plays" that cannot be attributed to Heywood with such certainty.

The knowledge it shows of medieval university exercises

and set terms goes far to support the story that the author was educated at a university.

THE ARGUMENT IN BRIEF

John argues the superiority of the Wise Man's life. James argues the ease and comfort of the Foolish Man's life and ends by making John "put his toong in his purs" by showing triumphantly that Fools not being responsible for their sins have a sure chance of heaven.

Then in true Morality style Jerome enters and shows that this plausible argument is untenable, and that wisdom triumphs in every way over folly.

It is amusing to see the way James unctuously lets his case fall to bits and gulps down wholesale the sententious dicta of Jerome.

THE ARGUMENT IN DETAIL

JAMES
Better ys for man that may be wyttles then wytty
Yn sewrty of lyvyng the sot doth remayne

JOHN
(*taking up the argument closely*)
In sewrty of lyvng but not without payne

John then narrates the miseries of the witless man.

The attention of the critic looking for internal evidence will be distracted particularly by the typically Heywoodian cumulations and the use of alliteration.

JOHN
Who cumeth by the sott who cumth he by
That vexythe hym not somewey usewally
Some beat hym some bob hym
Some joll hym some job hym
Some tugg hym by the hers
Some lugg hym by the eares

Some spet at hym some spurne hym
Some toss hym some turne hym
Some snap hym some scratch hym
Some cramp hym some cratch hym
Some cuff hym some clowt hym
Some lashe hym some lowte hym
Some whyske hym some whype hym
Wythe scharpe naylys some nype hym

He concludes typically:

Wyd wer the wytty to wysh them wyttles.

James admits that "the wyttles" suffers pain, but so does the wytty with his

Husband men's plowyng or earyng and sowyng
Hedgyng and dychyng with repyng and mowyng

so while

Sotts are coylde of other
The wytty coylthe hymself

and the sot is quite happy with his worthless "Walsyngam ryng."

For as I lode egally paynes of body
To wytty and wyttles lyke wyse wyll I
Overlode the wytty with payne of mynde

Later he concedes a point:

As good be wyttles as wytty say I.

John now takes him up ironically:

That *conclewsion* ys *conclewdyd* wysely
Your *pryme pr*oposycyon dyd *p*ut *pr*esysely
Better to be wyttles then wytty and now
As good to be wyttles as wytty sey yow
But that wytt whych putth case in *degre comparatyve*
And conclewdyth case in *degre posytyve*
Sal not in that case clame *degre sewperlatyve*

THE FINAL PAGE OF THE MS. "WYTTY AND WYTTLES" INCLUDING
THE SIGNATURE OF THE AUTHOR

JAMES

Ye pas in this tawnt yowr prerogatyve.

*   *   *   *   *

And so the barren dialogue goes on, till Jerome enters, who had "harde the pryncypall that plantyd thys jar." He asks James: "Whether wold ye be a resonable man or an unresonabyll beast?" For John grants that the "wyttles" and the beast are as one.

JEROME

Thynk yow the nombere
Standth as Somers dothe all day yn slomber
Nay Somers ys a sot folle for a kyng

He points out that everyone must make the most of his talents: that "one starr dyfferthe from another in shynyng"; and that all will be proportionately rewarded.

Of course, John is easily convinced by these highly respectable sentiments:

I woold now rather be
Sage Saloman than sot Somer I assewr ye.

All is therefore right with the morality of the world; and the interlude concludes with "Thes thre stave next folowyng" which "in the kyngs absens ar voyde." The three staves praise "our most loved and drade supreme soferayne, of this hye sort and hy hed most exelent"; and the author hopes that all present will obtain a high degree of bliss.

*   *   *   *   *

The play is of interest to the student for many reasons, e.g. for the information it gives about Heywood's place in early English drama, and about the type of amusement that appealed to the early sixteenth century.

I should like, however, to draw more particular attention to certain internal evidences, e.g.:

(i) to the constant use of "university" terms: e.g. "school-man," "commoner," "prime proposition," "principal";

(ii) to the Moralistic conclusion;

(iii) to the closeness of the Debate;

(iv) to the affected use of Alliteration:

> (*a*) James, John, and Jerome significantly forming the three *J*'s,
> (*b*) a mervelus mater, marcyful lord;

(v) to the Cumulation of lines of the same type, each line elaborately alliterated;

(vi) to the partisan attacks upon Will Summers, to whom Heywood must have thought himself very superior;

(vii) to the use of Proverbs and catchphrases;

(viii) to the pedantic humour:

> (*a*) Ye show some witty wyttiness;
> (*b*) Ye, but wytty and wytles wyttly wrowght;
> (*c*) That conclewsion ys conclewdyd wysely
> Your pryme proposycyon dyd put presysely
> Better to be wytles then wytty and now
> As good to be wyttles as wytty sey yow
> But that wytt whych putth case in degre cōparatyve
> And conclewdyth case in degre posytyve
> Sall not in that case clame degre sewperlatyve;
> (*d*) I thynk yowself wyll affyrme affyrmashyon.

*　　*　　*　　*　　*

This internal evidence throws light upon the authorship of those plays whose ascription to Heywood may still be doubted by a few critics, whose number is decreasing steadily.

II

A PLAY OF LOUE

A newe and a mery Enterlude
concernyng pleasure and payne in loue
made by Jhon Heywood
Pryntyd by W. Rastell
M.CCCCC.XXX.iii
cum Priuilegio

THE next play in order of merit and probably of time is also
one which by external and internal evidence undoubtedly
comes from the hand of Heywood.

The text given in the edition by Alois Brandl,[1] 1898, is
nearly faultless.

The text I have used is from the *editio princeps* in the
Library of Magdalene College, Cambridge.

The "play" introduces four characters:

> The Louer Loued
> The Louer not Beloued
> Neither Louer nor Loued
> The Woman Beloued not Louing.

The reader will gather at once with regret from the names and
initials of the *dramatis personae* (i.e. the Four L's) that there
is going to be much logic-chopping and hair-splitting.

But this play of sixteen hundred lines is an advance on
Wytty and Wyttles. For instance, it introduces a double
"debate."

> Who that lyst to marke
> Shall perceyue here a praty peyche of warke
> Let vs fall somewhat in these partes to skannyng
> Louyng not loued loued not louyng

[1] *Quellen des weltlichen Dramas in England vor Shakespeare.*

Loued and louyng not louyng nor loued
Wyll ye see these foure partes well ioyned
Louyng not loued and loued not louyng
Those partes can ioyne in no maner rekenyng
Louyng and loued loued nor louer   etc.

*   *   *   *   *

THE ARGUMENT IN BRIEF

The Louer not Beloued is the first to speak. In a long
speech he explains:

As *one* person to me is euerych*one*
So euery place to me but as *one*
And for that *one* persone euery place seke I
Whiche *one ones* founde I fynde of all the rest
Not *one* myssyng

and again:

No *tyme* can *tyme* my sewt to ease my wo
Before none to erely and all *tymes* els to late
Thus *tyme* out of *tyme* mys*tymeth* my rate
For *tyme* to brynge *tyme* to hope of any grace
That *tyme* *tyme*yth no *tyme* in any *tyme* or place
Wherby tyll *tyme* haue *tyme* so farre extyncte
That deth may determyne my lyfe thus dedly
No *tyme* can I reste

and:

Of all paynes the most incomparable payne
Is to be a louer not loued agayne

And so the "Debate, Strif or Estrif" opens, and the modern
reader begins to yawn. The Woman Beloued not Louing
replies:

Ye be a louer no whyt loued agayne
And I am loued of whome I loue nothyng
Then standyth our question betwene these twayne
Of louing not louyed or louyd not louing
Which is the case most paynfull in sufferyng
Wherto I saye that the moste payne doth moue
To those belouyd of whome they cannot loue

*   *   *   *   *

So the dialogue proceeds wearily; and in the manner and terminology of the Debate Louer not Loued asks:

> What can ye say nowe I come to *denyeng* your *princyple*

Then with typical abruptness and with much relief to the strain the "Louer belouyd entreth with a songe," followed a few lines later by Neither Louer nor Loued.

Louer Beloued states of Neither Louer nor Loued:

"This losell by lyke hath lost his wit," and concludes "the hyest pleasure that man may obtayne is to be a louer beloued agayne."

Neither Louer or Loued declares that he will prove him in his "*conclusion* before all this flock as wyse as a woodcocke," and adds very much in the manner of the Fool in *Twelfth Night*, and almost exactly in the manner of *The Foure P.P.* (*ad finem*):

> Wyll ye gyue me leaue to call ye fole anone
> When yourselfe perceyueth I have proued you one
> I am no louer in such maner ment
> As doth appeare in this purpose present
> For as touchyng women go where I shall
> I am at one poynt with women all
> The smothest the smyrkest the smallest
> The trewest the trymest the tallest
> The wysest the wylyest the wyldest
> The meryest the manerlyest the myldest
> The strangest the strayghtest the strongest
> (*and so on through eight more lines*)
> Take these with all the reste and of euerychone
> So god be my helpe I loue neuer one

Also he confirms his attitude by narrating in an amusing and Chaucerian story how he was fooled by a woman. This is the best and most lively thing in the piece. I advise my readers to read this, warning them that if it were a modern film it would be categorised as "A."

And so in the significant language of the play the "co-disputants" continue their "debate" with hair-splitting dis-

tinctions, logical terms, ponderous puns, and alliteration.
Louer Loued:

> For touchyng contentacyon I am in rate
> As hyely contented to loue as ye see
> As ye to forbere loue can wysh to be
> Had I no more to say in this argument
> But that I am as well as you content
> Yet hath my parte now good approbacyon
> To match with yours euen by contentacyon
> But contentacyon is not all the thyng
> That I for my loue haue in recompensyng
> Aboue contentacyon pleasures felyng
> Haue I so many . . . etc.

Neither Louer nor Loued:

> Syr though the effecte of your pleasure present
> Be more pleasaunt then displeasure absent
> Yet howe compare ye with myne absent payne
> By present displeasures in whiche ye remayne

*   *   *   *   *

At last a pathetically naïve bit of "business" is introduced
and most welcome it is:

Here the vyse cometh in ronynge sodenly aboute the place among
the audyens with a hye copyn tank on his hed full of squybs fyred
cryeng water water fyre fyre fyre water water fyre tyll the fyre in the
squybs be spent

Neither Louer nor Loued tells Louer Loued falsely that
the latter's house is afire. The victim of this practical joke
is distraught and the player of it claims that he has proved
his point. So presently the play concludes on a moralistic
note:

> Let us seke the loue of that louyng lorde
>
> *   *   *   *   *
>
> That it may please hym be mercyfull hearyng
> Thestate of this audyens longe to endure
> In myrth, helth, and welth to graunt his pleasure.
>
> Amen.

*   *   *   *   *

This play is one of the most tedious things in English literature except for those who can see the humour and the psychology of dullness. The allegory of *The Spider and the Flie* is very heavy going in parts; and *The Dialogue of Maryage* is often dull, but in *The Play of Loue*, except for a song irrelevantly introduced, and a pathetic bit of clowning with squibs and catcalls, and a humorous story told by one of the characters, there is nothing to relieve the monotony.

There is nothing approaching action on the stage and the speeches are long and precious.

The most one can say of it is that its characters are human beings and not abstractions. But it is an effort even to distinguish the permutations and combinations of their names.

However, the play is valuable for the light it throws upon what a Tudor audience could endure, and upon the technique of the Tudor playwright. In particular we may note:

(i) Once more the Debate and the Schoolman terminology;
(ii) The Cumulations;
(iii) The far-fetched Puns and Alliteration;
(iv) The forcible introduction of Proverbs.

All these seem to me to confirm beyond all doubt Heywood's authorship of the play and to give evidence on the other works commonly ascribed to him.

III

THE PLAY OF THE WETHER

A new and a very mery enterlude of al maner
wethers made by
John Heywood
Prynted by W. Rastell
1533
Cum Priuilegio

THIS is a third work which is attributed without doubt to
John Heywood.

It was printed by the younger Rastell in 1533. A copy of
this edition is in the Library of Magdalene College, Cambridge;
and another almost complete copy in the Library of St. John's
College, Oxford. There were at least two other editions, of
which one is in the Bodleian and another in the University
Library, Cambridge. The text here used is that of the *editio
princeps*.

Although here and there one can trace similarities between
this play and *Wytty and Wyttles* and *Loue* in words, technique, and construction, *The Play of the Wether*, primitive
as it is, makes them both appear earlier and amateurish. *The
Wether* is on the border-line of drama, a blend of debate and
farce; and it is shorter.

It is a true comedy and at the time when it was produced it
must have been very funny. It could, with abbreviation and
expurgation, be produced to-day. Indeed, I recollect its being
produced at a village in Cornwall some years ago.

THE ARGUMENT IN BRIEF

Jupiter in dignified language, with almost a Shakespearean
ring, declares that there has been a division in the gods' "hye

parlyament," mainly between Saturne, Phebus, Eolus, and Phebe. First of all, Saturne, his father

moste auncyent
Wyth berde whyte as snow, his lockes both cold & hore
Hath entred such mater as serued his entent
Laudynge his frosty mansyon in the fyrmament
To ayre & yerth as thynge most precyous
Pourgynge all humours that are contagyous

But Phebus with

His glarynge beamys maryth all in two howres.

Phebe wants "rayne"; while Eolus "when he is dysposed his blastes to blow, suffereth neyther soneshyne, rayne nor snow."

And as "can these IV in no maner agre," Jupiter declares that he is "now dyscendyd to satysfye all maner people whyche haue ben offendyd, by any wether mete to be amendyd."

*   *   *   *   *

In all the verses so far the reader will notice a refinement and a restraint and an absence of the artificiality, especially of forced Alliteration, and of the preciosity that mars *Wytty and Wyttles* and *Loue*.

*   *   *   *   *

The next character to enter is Meryreport, who is the Robin Goodfellow, or Puck of the piece. He never misses an opportunity to ridicule the foibles of humanity, to show what fools these mortals be, and with his tongue in his cheek to get them to take his joking seriously. If he cannot "put a girdle round the earth in forty minutes" he can mobilize all the characters before Jupiter in a very short time:

That shall be no lenger in doynge
Than I am in commyng and goynge

Jupiter asks who is this newcomer, and the dialogue is carried out in Heywoodian style.

MERYREPORT

Forsothe and please your lordshyppe it is I

JUPITER

All that we knowe very well but what I

MERYREPORT

What I Some saye I am I per se I
But what manner I so euer be I
I assure your good lordshyp I am I

Meryreport declares, in the cumulative manner:

For all wethers I am so indyfferent
Wythout affeccyon standynge so vpryght
Sonlyght monelyght sterlyght twylyght torchlight
Cold hete moyst drye hayle rayne frost snow lightnyng thunder
Cloudy mysty wyndy fayre fowle aboue head or vnder
Temperate or dystemperate whateuer yt be
I promyse your lordshyp all is one to me

*   *   *   *   *

So "Meryreport goth out. At th ende of this staf the god hath a song played in his trone or Meryreport come in."
The abruptness with which this song is introduced is paralleled with the introduction of the song in *Wytty and Wyttles*, of the Vice with the squibs business in *Loue*, of the second song in *The Wether*; and of the songs in *The Foure P.P.*

*   *   *   *   *

Jupiter now withdraws. In the idiom of Heywood he bids his audience "Reioyce ye in vs, wyth ioy most ioyfully."
Meantime Meryreport continues in the manner of Puck:

On my fayth I thynke in my conscyens
I haue ben from heuyn as farre as heuen is hens
At Louyn at London and in Lombardy
At Baldock at Barfolde and in Barbary

> At Canturberry at Couentre at Colchester
> At Wansworth Welbeck at Westchester
> At Fulham at Faleborne and at Fenlow

and so on for eleven lines with alliterations in W, T, G, H, S, W again, B, and G.

These lines are important for the prominence given to Louvain (cf. Louvain in *The Spider and the Flie*, Chapter 24, and in the Introduction on the life of Heywood), but more for the cumulative alliteration of which Heywood is so fond.

*　　　*　　　*　　　*　　　*

Now the Gentylman comes in and after a good deal of Chaucerian chaff, which is diverting, asks for

> wether pleasaunt
> Drye and not mysty the wynde calme and styll

Meryreport, with almost the same lack of technique by the playwright as is shown in his introduction of music and "business," turns the conversation on to one of his mountebank tricks:

> I can set my hedde and my tayle togyther
> This hed shall saue mony by saint mary
> From hensforth I wyll no potycary
> For at all tymys when suche thynges shall myster
> My new hed shall geue myne olde tayle a glyster[1]

*　　　*　　　*　　　*　　　*

This knock-about business would divert the audience until the argument was resumed and the Marchaunt comes in and asks for good sailing weather. Jupiter replies (this time in rhyme) that he is determined "iustely to iudge."

Next comes in the Ranger and asks for "a good rage of blustryng and blowynge" because he lives on the windfalls.

---

[1] In *The Foure P.P.* are found the same line endings, "myster" (master) and "glyster" (clyster).

But the Watermyller wants "plente of rayne"; while the Wyndmyller asks for "wynde contynuall."

  *   *   *   *   *

A close Debate begins between the two Millers, very much on the lines of *Wytty and Wyttles* and *Loue*; this time the debate is "Water *versus* Wind." I had almost written it "Water *wersus* Wind."

WATERMYLLER
Wherefore I thynke good before this audyens
Eche for ourselfe to say, or we go hens:
And whom is thought weykest when we haue fynysht
Leue of his sewt and content to be banysht

The Watermyller asks what a "shyppe" would do with wind and no water. The Wyndmyller retorts, What is the use of "a bagpype" filled with water? In Heywood's manner he backs his case with Proverbs: "And now to mynde there is one olde prouerbe come; one bushell of march dust is worth a kynges raunsome."

To this the Watermyller, when he can get a word in, replies in the manner of *Wytty* and *Wyttles*:

But now, syr, I deny your *pryncypyll*[1]

  *   *   *   *   *

Then at a difficult moment Meryreport interposes, like Jerome in *Wytty and Wyttles*—but in a very different vein, and in what critics of an age which is fortunately past called "the humour of filth."

His speech, in which one word is worried to death with many naughty innuendoes, probably ended in showers of laughter from the audience, who appreciated the contrast of his Rabelaisian humour with the dry dialectic of a few moments before.

[1] Again we must note the use of university and logical terms—principal, induction, case, conclude, etc.

E

Next "the Gentylwoman entreth," no doubt with a good deal of business. She is thinking of her complexion and wants "wether close and temperate" so that "she can jet the stretes trym as a parate."

> MERYREPORT
> Why sweteherte by your false fayth can ye syng
> Here they synge

*   *   *   *   *

Once more some relief by irrelevant and forced business.

*   *   *   *   *

And "Here the Launder cometh in," and after some badi- nage and crossing of swords with the fine lady, asks for sunshine so that she can dry her clothes.

> We can do ryght nought in our laundry
> Another maner losse if we sholde mys
> Then of such nycebyceters as she is[1]

When the Gentylwoman retires there is a short duel, this time between Meryreport and the Launder:

> The more ye byb the more ye babyll
> The more ye babyll the more ye fabyll
> The more ye fabyll the more vnstabyll
> The more vnstabyll the more vnabyll
>
> etc.[2]

Says Meryreport:

> I loue no launders that shrynke my gere in wettynge.

*   *   *   *   *

Then comes the most amusing scene in the play. "The

[1] For the odd word cf. Heywood's *Proverbes*, I, xi, 5. It may be a contraction of *Nescio quid Dicitur*.

[2] N.B. the same collocation of babble and fable in *The Pardoner and the Frere*, and elsewhere in Heywood's undoubted works.

✠ The Play of the wether.

❡A New and a very me=
ry enterlude of al maner we=
thers made by John
Heywood.

❡The players names.

☞ Jupiter a God.
☞ Mery report the vice
☞ The Gentylman.
☞ The marchaunt.
☞ The ranger.
☞ The water myller.
☞ The wynde Myller.
☞ The Gentylwoman.
☞ The Launder.
☞ A boy, the least that can play.

Boy comyth in, the lest that can play." In a naïve speech he asks for "plente of snow to make my snowballys."

> All my pleasure is in catchynge of byrdes
> And makynge of snowballys and throwyng the same
> For the whyche purpose to haue set in frame
> Wyth my godfather god I wolde fayne haue spoken
> Desyrynge to haue sent me by some token
> Where I myghte haue had great frosts for my pytfallys
> And plente of snow to make my snowballys
> This onys had boyes lyvis be such as no man leddys
> O to see my snow ballys lyght on my felowes heddys

*　　　*　　　*　　　*　　　*

The Debate is at an end. Jupiter summons all the suitors before him and sums up what he calls "the Debate" and in an odour of sanctity, and amid promises of snowballs from one of his grateful audience, states that he will do his best for everybody. He then ascends into heaven, and the play ends, no longer unexpectedly, with a song.

*　　　*　　　*　　　*　　　*

We have had a close Debate about Wind and Water. It is really a Debate within a Debate, because each character states the case for the weather that he wants.

Isolated words and rhymes confirm the single authorship of this and the other plays commonly ascribed to Heywood. And we have to note always the Heywoodian use of Cumulation, Alliteration, Proverbs, and Schoolman terms, the artificiality of the business; the collocation of "myster" and "glyster" and of "babyll" and "fabyll."

All of these minor and major evidences establish the authorship in particular of the trilogy of *The Pardoner and the Frere*, *The Foure P.P.*, and *Johan Johan*, which cannot be ascribed to Heywood so certainly.

IV

THE PARDONER AND THE FRERE

A mery play betwene
the pardoner and the frere, the curate and
neybour Pratte

Imprynted by Wyllyam Rastell
the v. day of Apryll
the yere of our lorde M
ccccc xxx iii

cum privilegio

THIS short play of a thousand lines is simply constructed of ribaldry and horseplay and from its crudity may well be the first of Heywood's true comedies.

There are only two copies of it and one of these is in the Library of Magdalene College, Cambridge. It was printed in 1533.

But it is necessary to examine it from internal evidence to prove what most people believe is correct, that it undoubtedly belongs to John Heywood.

Little doubt remains about the ascription of *The Foure P.P.* to Heywood. This play of the Pardoner, which is eventually a play of three P.P., treats the same subject—the faults of the established clergy and the atrocious impositions of religious mendicants with their spurious relics—in very much the same way, and often *in exactly the same language*, and apparently from the same source.[1]

I should therefore place this play in the trilogy of true comedies which are now commonly assigned to Heywood.

THE ARGUMENT IN BRIEF

The Frere comes on and his first words are significantly

[1] I.e. "The Pardoner's Tale" in *The Canterbury Tales*.

"Deus hic," just as in *The Foure P.P.* the first words of the play are "Now God be here"; and in *Johan Johan*, "God spede you maysters euerychone."

He explains, using a recognizable device:

> I com not hyther for meate nor for meale
> But I com hyther for your soules heale
> I com not hyther to poll nor to shaue
> I com not hyther to glose nor to flatter
> I com not hyther to bable nor to clatter
> I com not hyther to fable nor to lie[1]

*   *   *   *   *

He "than kneleth downe sayenge his prayers and in the meane whyle entreth the pardoner with all his reliques to declare what eche of them ben and the hole power and vertu thereof." In the exact *manner* of the Pardoner of *The Foure P.P.* he produces "the blessed arme of sweet saynt sondaye"; and in the exact *words* of *The Foure P.P.*, "the great too of the holy trynyte"; and "of all helowes the blessyd jaw bone."

There is a striking parallel of manner and matter between these two plays which cannot be neglected.

*   *   *   *   *

Meanwhile the Frere begins a sermon at the top of his voice, while the Pardoner at the top of his voice "begynneth also to shew and speke of his bullys and auctorytes com from Rome."

No doubt this shouting match, or Debate, was very amusing, especially when the words of one speaker accidentally overlapped the words of the other, and so a ridiculous sense was conveyed.

The dialogue continues in the style of Heywood's *Foure*

---

[1] It is convenient to stop the quotation here to draw attention to a collocation frequently used by Heywood, of "bable" and "fable." It is used again later on in this play. It is used in one of Heywood's undoubted plays, *Wether* ("the more ye babyll the more ye fabyll"). It is used again in the *Epigrammes*.

P.P., and the text of both speakers is "Give," till the match ends in hard words:

FRERE

By gogges soule knaue I suffre the no lenger

PARD

I say some good body lende me his hengar
And I shall hym teche by god almyght
How he shall another tyme lerne for to fyght
I shall make that balde crown of his to loke rede
I shall leue hym but one ere on his hede

FRERE

But I shall leue the neuer an ere or I go[1]

PARD

Ye horeson frere, wylt thou so

*　　*　　*　　*　　*

Than the fyght.[2] [*Much funny business!*]

*　　*　　*　　*　　*

FRERE

Lode thy handes away from myn earys

PARD

Than take thou thy handes away from my heres[3]

*　　*　　*　　*　　*

At this moment when they are "scrattyng and bytyng" the Parson and Prat—possibly the Prat of Heywood's *Epigrammes* (No. 66 of the "Fifth Hundred")—come in and

[1] The Frere had said earlier: "I shall lug the by the swete eares." Cf. (i) *Wytty and Wyttles*, "Some lugg hym by the eares"; and (ii) *Johan Johan*, also at end of play, "I shall make the blood ronne about his erys."
[2] Cf. *Johan Johan*, "Here they fyght by erys a whyle."
[3] Cf. *Wytty and Wyttles*, "Some tugg hym by the hers."

try and stop the fray (making of the four characters on the stage, a *P*ardoner, *P*arson, and *P*ratt, i.e. three P.P.).[1]

Prat takes on the Pardoner and the Parson takes on the Frere.

But they both bite off more than they can chew. Probably it was an artistic perversity that makes the pompous new-comers get the worst of it, with the "rede blood" soon running down their heads, just as "the red bloud runs down" in No. 58 of the "Three Hundred Epigrammes."

*   *   *   *   *

This play must have been very amusing when it was first produced. I consider that it is sufficiently good to be produced to-day; but I have vainly made overtures to managers. It has far more action than the three plays of Heywood which we have studied so far. Also the action is all relevant and the business is not forced in abruptly. The artistic determination is perhaps most remarkable.

The reader will admit presently the great similarity of this play to *The Foure P.P.*

It contains as usual a Debate but a Debate in a modern disguise which is not concluded by a sententious Jerome.

I notice a new artifice in the play—the use of two words, often at the end of a verse, to express the same idea, "to poll nor to shaue," "barefote and barelegged," "to begge nor to craue," "to fable nor to lye," "for grotes nor for pens," "my doctryne and connynge," "cursyd or paruert," "trew and juste," "whete or oates," "power and might," "grief nor pain," "crouche and crepe," "your doctryne and your lore," "mysery and payne." But perhaps this is not a peculiarly Heywoodian device.

---

[1] Cf. (i) the three *j*'s in *Wytty and Wyttles*. (ii) The three *j*'s in "Johan Johan and Syr Johan." (iii) *The Foure P.P.*; (iv) the four *l*'s in *Loue*; and (v) the three *m*'s in *The Spider and the Flie*.

A proverb is introduced entirely in Heywood's manner:

Marry that wolde I se quod blynde hew.

I consider, therefore, that (i) as the play will be found to treat much the same subject as *The Foure P.P.*, in much the same way, and often *verbatim*—and (ii) as the play begins with *Deus hic*, which is only a Latinized version of "God be with you," with which *The Foure P.P.* begins, and (iii) as it has the usual Heywoodian Debate for the mastery and all the devices that we have noted in Heywood's undoubted plays, including twice the collocation of "bable" and "fable"—that we must assign *The Pardoner and the Frere The Foure P.P.* to our author without uncertainty.[1]

---

[1] Some argument may be based on the reference, late in the play, to Pope Leo. But it is not clear that the reference is to a reigning monarch.

V

THE PLAYE CALLED THE FOURE P.P.

A newe and a very mery enterlude of a palmer,
a pardoner, a poticary a pedler made by

John Heewood

Imprynted at London in Flete strete
at the sygne of the George by Wyllyam
Myddylton

THIS is one of the most humorous of Heywood's plays.
Though perhaps reliant on the inspiration of contemporary
French farce, it is Chaucerian and English in sentiment and
just the kind of play suitable for an entertainment after a
Court dinner.

Three editions of it are extant and I have discussed them
with the text later.

It is ascribed to Heywood by the printer Myddylton, and
this ascription must be accepted unless reasonable cause or
impediment can be shown. I wish to confirm this ascription.

The Alliteration of the *dramatis personae*, the Palmer, the
Pardoner, the Poticary, and the Pedler, and the title *The
Foure P.P.* are typical of Heywood.[1]

THE ARGUMENT IN BRIEF

A Palmer enters and tells in burlesque of his many pilgrimages
to Jerusalem, "Iosophat and Olyuete," where "many a salt
tere dyde I swete." Many verses are taken up with the list of

---

[1] Cf. the *dramatis personae*, John, James, Jerome, in *Wytty and Wyttles*;
and in *Loue*; cf. too the Pardoner, the Parson, and Prat in *The Pardoner
and the Frere*; and Johan Johan and Sir Johan; and Margaret, Maria, and
Margery in *The Spider and the Flie*.

shrines he has visited. He even has been on the hills of Armenia, where he saw Noah's ark.

*   *   *   *   *

The intricate knowledge of shrines and relics, despite the humorous way in which it is couched, bears out the religious set of Heywood's mind.

*   *   *   *   *

The Pardoner retorts:

> And when ye haue gone as farre as ye can
> For all your labour and gostely entente
> Yet welcome home as wyse as ye wente

and

> What haue ye wone by ronnyng at Rome

and

> Geve me but a peny or two pens
> And as sone as the soule departeth hens
> In halfe an hour or thre quarters at moste
> The soule is in heuen with the Holy Ghost

Then the Poticary interrupts:

> And whom haue ye knowen dye ho [ne] stlye
> Without helpe of the potycary
> Nay all that commeth to our handlynge
> Except ye happe to come to hangynge
> That way perchaunce ye shall nat myster
> To go to heuen without a glyster[1]

Now the Pedler enters.

POTICARY
Were the deuyll were we foure hatched

PEDLER
That maketh no mater syns we be matched

---

[1] Cf. the similar line endings "myster" and "glyster" in Meryreport's speech in *Wether*. N.B. "glyster"—another form of "clyster"—recurs in *The Foure P.P.*

Then he displays his wares.

> Gloues pynnes combes glasses vnspottyd
> Pomanders hookes and lasses knotted
> Broches rynges and all maner bedes
> Lace rounde and flat for womens hedes
> Nedyls thredes thymbell shers and all suche knackes
> Where louers be no suche thynges lackes
> Sypers swathbondes rybandes and sleue laces
> Gyrdyls knyues purses and pyncases
>
> Frontlettes fyllettes parlettes and barcelettes
> And then theyr bonettes and theyr poynettes
> By these lettes and nettes the lette is suche
> That spede is small whan haste is muche[1]

Just as in *Wether*, Meryreport grossly ridicules the debaters, especially the Watermyller, so the Pedler's list of his wares is interrupted by a number of indecent puns in which one word "pynne" is worried to death; which must have sent the audience of that day into fits of laughter, though to-day the joke could hardly be printed and certainly not repeated publicly. The full text is given later.

Then comes a dialogue with "business" and mannerisms which we have now learnt to recognize. It is naïvely apropos of nothing.

POTIC.

Then tell me thys are you perfyt in drynkynge

PEDL.

Perfyt in drynkynge as may be wysht by thynkyng

POTIC.

Then after your drynkyng how fall ye to wynkyng

PEDL.

> Syr after drynkynge whyle the shot is tynkynge
> Some hedes be swymmyng byt myne wyl be synkynge
> And vpon drynkynge myne eyse wyll be pynkynge
> For wynkynge to drynkynge is alway lynkynge

[1] This is all in Heywood's manner, e.g. in *Wether* compare the lines beginning :"Sonlyght monelyght sterlyght twylyght torchlight."

POTIC.

I pray you tell me can you synge

*   *   *   *   *

Here they synge

The reader will recognize the way the rhyme is worried and the abruptness with which the song is forced in.

*   *   *   *   *

PARDONER

I aske but twopens at the moste
I wys this is nat very great coste
to get a man to heaven
And more then heuen he cannat get
How farre soeuer he lyste to iet[1]

The Poticary, the Palmer, and the Pardoner now propose the usual Heywoodian *Debate*—it is really a *second* Debate— and declare that the Pedler shall be referee,

Shall be our iudge as in thys case
Whiche of vs thre shall take the best place

The Pedler is indifferent and replies (significantly in the terminology of the university):

It behoueth no pedlers nor *proctours*
To take on them judgemente as *doctours*

However, he decides that:

sins ye canot agree in voyce
Who shal be hed there is no choyse
But deuyse some maner thynge

He suggests, therefore, that they have a lying competition, or "Mastry."

So once more we recognize the dramatic device of the Debate we have noticed in *Wytty and Wyttles, Wether,*

---

[1] The word "jet" is a conspicuous favourite with Heywood in the plays which we have examined so far.

Loue, and *The Pardoner and the Frere*. Of this many examples
are yet to be given.

*   *   *   *   *

"*Here the poticary hoppeth*"—just like Meryreport in
Wether, who shows for no reason that he can set his head and
tail together.

*   *   *   *   *

PALMER
Here were a hopper to hop for the rynge
But syr thys gere goth nat by hoppynge

POTIC.
Syr in this hopynge I wyll hop so well
That my tonge shall hop as well as my hele
Upon which hoppynge I hope and nat doute it
To hope so that ye shall hope without it

*   *   *   *   *

But before the Debate or "the Mastry" begins the Pardoner
shows his pardons and his relics (many of which are found
verbatim in *The Pardoner and the Frere*):

and
    of All-Hallows the blessyd iawbone

and
    the great toe of the trinite

and
    the buttocke bone of Pentecoste

and
    a slypper of one of the seuen slepers

and
    the eye toth of the great Turk

    a box full of humble bees
    That stonge Eue as she sat on her knees

*   *   *   *   *

The others ridicule him with coarse jokes that must have tickled a Tudor audience, and which make this play, even to-day, a great success. I wish that someone would venture to produce it.

* * * * *

The Poticary next shows his wares, diapompholicus ("Thys oyntement is euen shotankor") and alkakengy ("a good thynge for dogges that be mangy"), "Mercury sublyme and metridaticon, cassy and colloquintita."

So after much dialectic and hair-splitting on the word "lye" they get on with a Mastery which is the biggest liar.

* * * * *

The Poticary tells a very Rabelaisian yarn, which I dare not repeat, how he cured a young woman with "a glyster," the usual Heywoodian remedy, which was unexpectedly and ruinously successful.

* * * * *

The Pardoner tells a more decent yarn how he recovered a woman client from hell. This is jolly and quite in the manner of *The Ingoldsby Legends*, and must be read in the full text.

All the deuyls of hell togyther
Strode in aray in suche apparell
As for that day there metely fell
Theyr hornes well gylt theyr clowes full clene
Theyr taylles well kempt and as I wene
With sothery butter theyr bodyes anoynted
I neuer saw deuyls so well appoynted
The mayster deuyll sat in his iacket
And all the soules were playnge at racket

The teller of the story had been taken by Lucifer into Hell's kitchen; and there was Margery (one of Heywood's favourite names)

> bysely turnynge of the spyt
> For many a spyt here heth she turned
> And many a good spyt hath she burned

So the Pardoner

> toke her fro the spyt for speed

and brought her to Newmarket Heath.

*　　　*　　　*　　　*　　　*

It is now the Palmer's turn. He says that he is surprised to hear in the Pardoner's tale how delighted the devils were to get rid of Margery, and "how the cheynes in hell dyd rynge and how all the soules therin dyd synge" because

> In all the places where I haue ben
> Of all the women that I haue sen
> I neuer sawe nor knewe in my consyens
> Any one woman out of paciens

*　　　*　　　*　　　*　　　*

The stories are done, and the Pedler now considers his verdict which is the greatest liar. He decides

> Yf ye (the poticary) had sayd ye had made fle
> Ten tampyions out of ten womens tayles
> Ten tymes ten myle to ten castels or tayles
> And fyll ten ryuers ten tymes so depe
> As ten of that whiche your castell stones dyde kepe
> Or yf ye (the pardoner) ten tymes had bodely
> Fet ten soules out of purgatory
> And ten tymes so many out of hell
> Yet by these ten bonnes I could ryght well
> Ten tymes sonner all that haue beleued
> Than the tenth parte of that he (the palmer) hath meved[1]

So after a great deal more play on "ten" the Palmer gets the verdict.

---

[1] Cf. the use of "meved" in *Johan Johan* and elsewhere.

For, says the Pedler:

> Amonge the women in thys border
> Take thre of the yongest and thre of the oldest
> Thre of the hotest and thre of the coldest
> Thre of the wysest and thre of the shrewdest
> Thre of the chastest and thre of the lewdest
> Thre of the lowest and thre of the hyest

—and so on for several more lines (unmistakably in Heywood's spirit, both for manner and matter)

> Of eche thre two iustly by nomber
> Shall be founde shrewes except thys fall
> That ye hap to fynde them shrewes all[1]

*   *   *   *   *

The Debate is over, and the play closes as was usual on a moralizing note.

*   *   *   *   *

I have no doubt in ascribing this play to Heywood. I base this ascription on:

(i) the ascription of the play to Heywood by Wyllyam Myddylton;

(ii) the Alliteration of the names of the *dramatis personae*;

(iii) the pedantic Alliteration of the verses;

---

[1] Cf. a striking parallel in *Loue*:

> "For as touchyng women go where I shall
> I am at one poynt with women all
> The smotest the smyrkest the smallest
> The trewest the trymest the tallest
> The wysest the wylyest the wyldest
> The strangest the strayghtest the strongest
> *   *   *   *   *
> The syntlyest the sewrest the syckest
> Take these with all the reste and of euerychone
> So god by my helpe I loue neuer one"

F

(iv) the word-worrying and the hair-splitting dialectic;

(v) the constant introduction of Proverbs;

(vi) the constant use of the Debate;

(vii) the similarity between Meryreport in *Wether* and the Poticary; both are acrobats and both are indecent in their remarks in their efforts to ridicule others;

(viii) the collocation again of "myster" and "glyster";

(ix) the attitude to women;

(x) and the similarity of many passages in this play with passages in the plays we have already studied and ascribed.

I have no doubt that it is a genuine Heywood play, although it is far and away superior to the plays which we have examined hitherto; and I recommend it to the reader.

It is a successful comedy and very amusing to read. Still, in spite of this superiority, the only actions of the play are a song and some acrobatic turns artificially introduced.

The ascription of this play is important in determining the authorship of *Johan Johan* as well as of *The Pardoner*.[1]

---

[1] For the display of relics cf. "The Pardoner's Tale" (in *The Canterbury Tales*), which also introduces a Potecary.

VI

JOHAN JOHAN

A mery play betwene Johan Johan the husbande Tyb his wife
and Syr Jhan the preest
Impryntyd by Wyllyam Rastell the xii
day of February the yere of our lord
M ccccc and xxxiii
Cum priuilegio.

THIS is the best and probably the latest of Heywood's farces.
It is only seven hundred lines long. Part of it is probably
borrowed—like, perhaps, parts of the other plays—from
contemporary French farce. But its final character is English.

The only known edition is in the Pepys Collection of Magdalene College, Cambridge; of which there is another copy in the
Bodleian.

It is one of the plays commonly ascribed to Heywood, and
I wish to confirm this ascription for several reasons.

It opens with the henpecked husband descanting on what
he will do to his wife when she comes home.

> By our lady of crome
> I wolde bete her or that I drynke
> Bete her q[uo]da yea that she shall stynke
> And at euery stroke lay her on the grounde
> And trayne her by the here about the house rounde
> I am euyn mad that I bete her not nowe
> But I shall rewarde her hardly well ynowe
> There is neuer a wyfe betwene heuen and hell
> Whiche was euer beten halfe so well
> Beten quoda but what and she thereof dye
> Then I may chaunce to be hanged shortly
> And whan I haue beten her tyll she smoke
> And gyven her many a C. stroke

> Thynke ye that she wyll amende yet
> Nay by our lady the deuyll spede whyt
> Therfore I wyll not bete her at all
> And shall I not bete her no shall . . .
> Shall I not bete her if she do so
> Yes by cokkes blood that shall I do
> I shall bete her and thwak her I trow

The word "bete" is used over twenty times in this opening tirade.

But when his wife suddenly enters, of course before he is aware of her entrance, and while he is finishing his diatribe, he sings a very different tune and says:

> Well let vs have no more debate

The wife tells her husband that she and her "gossyp Margery" (a favourite name with Heywood) have made a pie and she dispatches her husband to pray "Syr Johan the preest" to come and sup with them that night.

JOHN

> Nowe a vengaunce and a very myschyefe
> Lyght on the pylde preest and on my wyfe
> On the pot the ale and on the table
> The candyll the pye and all the rable
> On the trystels and on the stole
> It is moche ado to please a curst fole
>
> Nay than if my wyfe be set a-chydyng
> It is tyme for me to go at her byddyng
> There is a prouerbe which trewe nowe preueth
> He must nedes go that the dyuell dryueth[1]

*   *   *   *   *

Johan Johan then trots off to Sir Johan, the priest.[2] Sir

---

[1] N.B.—Heywoodian mannerism, cf. *Wether*, "And now to mynde there is one olde prouerbe come."

[2] This time it is the three *j*'s again; cf. three *j*'s in *Wytty and Wyttles*; in *Loue*, the four *l*'s; *The Foure P.P.*; the three *m*'s.

Johan tells Johan Johan the husband that there is "a Debate" between him, Sir Johan, and the woman because he advises against her will

> She is angry with me and hath me in dysdayn
> Because that I do her oft intyce
> To do some penaunce after myne aduyse
> Because she wyll neuer leue her wrawlyng
> But alway with the she is chydyng and brawlyng
> And therfore I knowe she hatyth me presens

He convinces the suspicious husband that he is trying—in the phrase used twice at least in *The Spider and the Flie*—to "stynt the debate" between Johan Johan and his wife; and so he is persuaded to join the supper-party at Johan Johan's house.

Tyb's first words to her husband when he returns are:

> The deuyll take the for thy longe taryeng
> Here is not a whyt of water by my gowne
> To washe our handes that we myght syt downe
> Go and hye the as fast as a snayle
> And with fayre water fyll me this payle

While the cuckold fetches water, the Priest says:

> By god I wolde ye had harde the tryfyls
> The toys the mokkes the fables and the nyfyls
> That I made thy husbande to beleue and thynke[1]

At this point the husband re-enters with an empty pail and declares that there is a hole in it. His shrew wife tells him to chafe two wax candles and use the melted wax to stop the leak.

Johan Johan grumbles:

> Nowe so god helpe me and by my holydome.[2]

He is at the fire. His wife and the Priest are at the table. The

---

[1] This unusual word "nyfyls" is found in *Wether*, when it is again found in company with "tryfyls."

[2] Cf. in *Wether*: "So helpe me god and holydome."

dialogue, in which the words "chafe the waxe" endlessly recur like the drone of a bagpipe, is too long to be quoted here. But there is a great similarity in this bit of dialogue and the dialogue between the Pardoner and the Friar, in which there was a similar droning with the recurrence of two words.

Meantime the shrew and the Priest are enjoying themselves tucking away the pie, while the Priest tells doubtful stories.

At last Johan Johan, exasperated, bursts out:

> But howe say you syr Johan was it good your pye
> The dyuell the morsell that thereof eate I
> By the good lorde this is a pyteous warke
> But nowe I see well the olde prouerbe is trew
> The parysshe preest forgetteth that euer he was clarke[1]

*   *   *   *   *

Hard knocks soon follow hard words, and we hear that "blood will be ronnyng aboute the erys," just as at the close of *The Pardoner and the Frere* "blood was running about the head," and just as in the *Epigrammes* "red blood runs down the cheek."

*   *   *   *   *

"*They fyght by the erys awhyle*"; just as the Frere threatened to lug the Pardoner by "the swete eares" and says later when they fight: "I shall leve the neuer an ere."[2]

*   *   *   *   *

This play is another advance on *The Pardoner and the Frere* and *The Foure P.P.* There is a plot and much lively action.

The *motif*, too, is new. The Church has almost been driven off the stage. It is a shrew play.

Though the Debate is frequently used, it is always kept

---

[1] A proverb which occurs twice more in Heywood's undoubted works and is introduced here in Heywood's usual manner.

[2] Cf. *Wytty and Wyttles*: "Some lugg hym by the eares."

latent. There is less pedantic Alliteration and no logic-chopping.

In conclusion I consider that the play must be attributed to Heywood, though I can only base my opinion on rather small evidences:

(i) that this play, like *The Pardoner and the Frere*, ends in a free fight;

(ii) that in the trilogy, *The Pardoner and the Frere, The Foure P.P., Johan Johan*, the attitude to women is the same;

(iii) that the first words of all three plays are almost identical;

(iv) that all three plays contain in a greater or less degree a Debate;

(v) that there are similarities in dialogue between this play and *The Pardoner and the Frere*;

(vi) that two Proverbs, which occur again in an undoubted work of Heywood, are forcibly introduced in Heywood's manner;

(vii) that words like "meve" and "nyfyls," which are Heywoodian words, are introduced;

(viii) that in both *The Pardoner and the Frere* and in *Johan Johan*, the play ends in a *fight by the ears*;

(ix) that one constantly gets in this play as in *The Pardoner and the Frere* two words at the end of a line to express one idea, e.g. "pastime and sport," "done and past," "woe and pain," "set and laid," "chiding and brawling."[1]

With this evidence, though I admit it is weak, and from this general character of the play I consider that we are justified in accepting the traditional canon.

[1] Further notes: (i) "Margery" recurs in *The Foure P.P.* and in *The Spider and the Flie* as the name of a character; (ii) the proverb about the parish priest occurs *three times* in Heywood's works—twice in undoubted works from Heywood; (iii) the three *j*'s of the play.

VII

DIALOGUE

A DIALOGUE conteyning the number of the effectuall prouerbes in
the Englishe tounge compact in a matter concernynge two maner
of maryages
Londini Anno Christi 1562

This *Dialogue* has been accurately reprinted by the Spenser
Society (1867) from the original 1562 edition, collated with
the second 1566 edition, and with an appendix of variations.

It throws valuable light upon the authorship of other
work not certainly ascribed to Heywood.

It is on this *Dialogue*, the *Epigrammes,* and perhaps on the
allegory of *The Spider and the Flie* that Heywood's contemporary fame was most strongly based. He probably prided
himself most on these works. He may have felt that the scope
of drama was smaller.

The *Dialogue* is divided into two parts and Part 1 begins
with a preface dealing with the value of "our common plaine
pithie prouerbes olde," and the author's intent "that the
reader redily may finde them and minde them whan he wyll
alway."

THE ARGUMENT IN BRIEF

It is divided into thirteen chapters. Chapter 1 relates how a
young man came for advice to the writer, whether he should
marry a poor maid with rich friends, or a rich widow with
poor friends, i.e. a maid of flowering age or a white-haired
widow—a truly Heywoodian antithesis.

In Chapter II the writer compliments the young man on his
wisdom in taking advice of another: for

> Sage sayings dooe weightily way
> Against hast in all thing but I am at bay
> By other parables of like weightie weight
> Which hast me to weddyng as ye shall here streight

In Chapter III he continues:

> Whan the sunne shinth make hay which is to say
> Take time when time comth lest time steale away
> And one good lesson to this purpose I pike
> From the smithis forge whan thyron is hot strike
> The sure seaman seeth the tide tarieth no man
> And long delayes and absence somwhat to skan
> Sens that that one will not on other will
> Delaie in woers must needes their speede spill
> And touchyng absence the full accompte wo somth
> Shall see as fast as one goth another comthe
> Time is tickell and out of sight out of minde
> Then catche and holde while I may fast binde fast finde

In Chapter VII—that is after all this stringing together of Proverbs, often with a forcedness and disconnection—the writer narrates to the young seeker after advice, how in the same city "two yong men were abydyng," one of whom married a poor, good-looking maid and the other a rich, ugly widow. The poor maid's looks soon faded with trouble, and her husband came to the writer to ask for advice. The writer advised him to go to his rich uncle and to send his wife to her rich aunt.

Both errands ended disastrously. Both came back insulted and not a penny the better off; so to avoid starvation they had to seek service—and were driven asunder many miles.

> And thus by loue without regard of liuyng
> These twayne haue wrought eche others yll chiuyng
> And loue hath so lost them the loue of their freendis
> That I thinke them lost and thus this tale eendis

*   *   *   *   *

Part II tells the tale of the young man who married a rich crone.

She was made "lyke a beerepot, or a barell, a crooked hooked nose, beetyll-browde, blere eyde." However, all began well. Then

> sens all thyng is the woors for the wearyng
> Decaie of cleane sweepyng folke had in fearyng
> And indede er two monthes away were crept,
> And hir biggest baggs into his bosome swept,
> Where loue had apeered in him to hir alway
> Hotte as a toste, it grew cold as a kay
> He at meate caruyng hir and none els before
> Now carued he to all but hir and hir no more

So the young man came for advice to the writer, who smoothed over their difficulties for the moment. But the unmatched couple "soon fell at a newfrey"—and first the young man and then the old lady came by night secretly to consult the writer and to air their grievances.

The upshot was (because here the story becomes tedious):

> Thus *w*are and *w*asted this most *w*ofull *w*retche
> Tyll death from this lyfe did hir wretchedly fetche
> Her late husbande and now wydower here and there
> Wandryng about few know and fewer care where
> Caste out as an abiect he leadeth his lyfe
> Tyll famine bylyke fet him after his wyfe

*   *   *   *   *

And the moral of it all was:

> Thus failed all foure of all thinges lesse and more
> Whiche they all or any of all maryed fore

Thereupon the young man who came for advice and to whom were told the fates of the other two young men says:

> But marke how foly hath me away caryed
> First these two women to loose I was so lothe
> That if I might I woulde have wedded them *bothe*
> Than thought I sens to have wedded *one* of them
> And now know I cleere I will wed *none* of them
> They both shall haue this one aunswere by letter
> As good neuer a whit as neuer the better

*   *   *   *   *

All these Proverbs bound up in a story no doubt were as amusing to a contemporary reader as to the author. They are much commended by Thomas Wilson in *Arte of Rhetorike*, London, 1553.[1] They are not without interest for the light they throw upon the society of Heywood's day.

But on the whole the *Dialogue* makes tedious reading, except to the students of humour and of dramatic evolution, and one welcomes the little oases of incident where precept is not piled upon precept.

To me it is of most interest as showing, not merely what Heywood's age could endure, but what it could enjoy.

And do not forget that we have still to consider the *Epigrammes* and the *Allegory*—stiff bunkers for the modern reader to carry.

*   *   *   *   *

About the authorship of the *Dialogue* there is no doubt. It was one of Heywood's most notable works. On the other hand, one can extract internal evidence from it which has a bearing on the authorship of work which is not ascribed to him so certainly.

E.g., in the *Dialogue* occur the lines:

> Where wooers hoppe in and out long time may bryng
> Him that hoppeth best at last to haue the ryng
> I hoppyng without for a ryng of a rushe
> And while I at length *debate* . . .

and in *The Foure P.P.* in the middle of a "mastry" or Debate, the Palmer says:

> Here were a hopper to hop for the rynge
> But syr thys gere goth nat by hoppynge

Again, in the *Dialogue* occur the words:

> Her substaunce is shoote anker

---

[1] The earliest edition of the *Proverbs* is believed to be 1546.

And in *The Foure P.P.* the words:

Thys oyntement is euen shotankor

The word also recurs in *The Spider and the Flie.*

Again, the word "jet"—a favourite in Heywood's undoubted plays and in these Proverbs—is found several times
in *The Foure P.P.*, cf. also "meve."

*   *   *   *   *

So much for the evidence that affects the question of the
authorship of *The Foure P.P.*

As regards *The Pardoner and the Frere*, we note in Chapter vi, Part ii, of the *Proverbs* the old collocation of "fabling"
and "babbling" about which I have argued before, and to
which I shall draw attention again in the *Epigrammes.*

*   *   *   *   *

But the strongest evidence of this sort that I can produce
has to do with *Johan Johan*, of which the ascription is the
least easy.

In Chapter v of Part ii of the *Proverbs* there is a reference
"to that cunnyng man our curate, sir John."

The character, the profession, and the name remind us irre-
sistibly of Sir Johan in *Johan Johan*; more especially as in the
Proverbs the woman who is speaking says about her unfor-
tunate marriage,

And for counsaile herein, I thought to haue gone
To that cunnyng man, our curate, Sir John.

And in the play *Johan Johan*, the shrew wife says of Sir Johan
the priest:

Mary he is my curate I say
My confessour and my frende alway

and the priest tells Johan that he is always giving her advice
about how to make the best of her marriage.

In Chapter I of Part II of the *Proverbs* occurs the verse about the young man who married the elderly, ugly lady who financed the house:

> Now carued he to all but hir and hir no more

In the same way in *Johan Johan* the pie was carved to everyone except the master of the house.

Again in Chapter XI of Part I of the *Proverbs* occur the lines:

> For the paryshe priest forgetteth
> That euer he hath bene holy water clarke

And in the *Johan* play occur the lines:

> But howe say you syr Johan was it good, your pye
> The dyuell the morsell that therof eate I
> By the good lorde this is a pyteous warke
> But nowe I se well the old prouerbe is treu
> Thet parysshe preest forgetteth that euer he was clarke

This Proverb recurs also in the *Epigrammes*.

Similarly we can compare with the verse in Chapter XI of Part II of the *Dialogue*:

> He hath a pyg of the woorse panier

the verse in the conclusion of *Johan Johan*:

> Then had I a pyg in the worrs panyer

I think these not very strong similarities go to confirm the ascription to John Heywood of *Johan Johan*.

VIII

THE EPIGRAMMES

(i) The Firste Hundred of Epigrammes. Inuented and made by John Heywood.

Londini   1562

(ii) Three Hundred Epigrammes upon Three Hundred Prouerbes, inuented and made by John Heywood.

Londini   .   1562

(iii) The Fifth Hundred of Epygrams. Inuented and made by John Heywood.

Londini   Anno Christi

1562

(iv) A Sixt Hundred of Epigrammes. Newly inuented and made by John Heywood.

Londini   Anno Christi

1562

Imprinted at London in Fleete strete by
Thomas Powell
Cum Priuilegio.

THESE *Epigrammes* have been reprinted accurately by the Spenser Society (1867) from the original edition (1562) and collated with the second edition (1566), with an appendix of variations.

Upon them the fame of John Heywood mainly rested. They give internal evidence on all sorts of points and not least on what could tickle the fancy of the sixteenth century.

In the *Epigrammes* we have "a thyn trym trencher" on which, says A. W. Ward, in his introduction to *The Spider and the Flie*, 1899, "we are served with a light, palatable and, here and there, pungent banquet." The writer sets out "not to teach but to touch."

An idea of their quality can be gained from a few quotations. I quote from "The Firste Hundred":

of three sages.   2.

Three maner sages nature dooth deuise
The sage herbe the sage foole and the sage wise
And who for moste wyse him selfe dooth accept
Maie matche any sage the sage wise except

Of the wyues and hir husbandes waste.   35.

Where am I least husband quoth he in the wast
Which comth of this thou art vengeable streit laste
Where am I biggest wife in the waste (quoth shee)
For all is waste in you as far as I see

Of two studentes.   46.

Two scolers yonge in the vniuersitee late
Kept in thinne diet after scolars rate
Thone beyng an eater greedy and greate
Thother a weake feeder said at his meate
Oh this smart small pittans and hungrie diet
Maketh us to studie aptly and quiet
    Sure (said the tother) small meales are induction
To thencrease of studie for deper instruction
This diner shall driue me to studie anon
Where I maie get more meate whan this is gon

An olde widower and a yong mayde.   66.

A widower riche with riueld face old
Wooyng a fayre yong woman his minde he told
Bostyng what he had as wowers doe that can
Wherin he bosted of a goodly yong man
A son of his owne whome god had him sent
Of condicions and qualitees excellent
In this whot wooyng this old mans behauour
So far foorth had won this yong womans fauour
That in short tale whan his long tale was don
She prayd him to go home and send hir his son

A wiues defence of hir beetill brow.   79.

Were I to wed againe wife I make a vow
I would not wed a wife with a beetill brow
And I (quoth she) rather would a husband wed
With a beetill brow than with a beetell hed

*   *   *   *   *

I quote from the "Three Hundred Epigrammes":

Takyng hart of grasse.   92.

Thou takest hart of grasse wyfe not hart of grace
Cum grasse cum grace syr we grase both in one place

Measure.   128.[1]

Measure is mery meane
Which filde with noppy drinke
When mery drinkers drinke of cleane
Then merely they winke[2]

Of the foxes preaching.   166.

When the foxe preacheth then beware our geese
You that feare your geese learne wyt here a peese
Kepe foxes from pulpets your geese to teache
Or kepe geese from sermons when foxes do preache

*   *   *   *   *

I quote from "The Fifth Hundred of Epygrams":

Of a sharpe tunge.   5.

Wife I perceiue thy tunge was made at Egeware
Ye sir and yours made at Rayly harde by thare

Of a yong wooer.   72.

I brought the late an olde riche widow to woo
Whom thou mightst haue had but nought woldst thou the[n] doo

---

[1] Of this there are ten variations in the manner of Thomas More's
Epigrams.
[2] Cf. in *Foure P.P.*, "Wynkynge to drynkynge is alway lynkynge."

Nor nought canst thou do now thrift and thou art od
For now lieth she speechless at mercy of god
For the mercy of god bring me now to hir
I never sawe meete time till nowe to woo hir

*   *   *   *   *

Finally from this section I quote an epigram which is of great importance in the ascription of the plays.

Of Heywood. 100.

Art thou Heywood with the mad mery wit
Ye forsooth maister that same is euen hit
Art thou Heywood that applieth mirth more then thrift
Ye sir I take mery mirth a golden gift
Art thou Heywood that hath made many mad plaies
Ye many plaies fewe good woorkes in all my daies
Art thou Heywood that hath made men mery long
Ye and will if I be made mery among
Art thou Heywood that woulde be made mery now
Ye sir helpe me to it now I beseche yow

*   *   *   *   *

From the "Sixt Hundred" I quote:

Of Rebellion. 1.

Against god I dayly offend by frailte
But against my prince or natiue countre
With as much as bodkin when I rebell
The next daie after hang me vp faire and well
The next daie after nay the next daie before
Wishe thou thy selfe hangd in that case euermore
Before thou hangst honestly unwoorthyly
After thou hangst woorthyly unhonestly
But ho at our fyrst dyshe in our mery feast
Why talke we of hangyng our myrth to molest
Be our cheese no better than our pottage is
Better fast than feast at such feastes as is this
But beyng true to god queene countre and crowne
We shall at all feastes not hang up but syt downe

G

Of a waterman's rowyng.   32.

Thy fares ouer the water thou shouldst row them
But vnder the water thou doost bestow them

A question to a childe.   50.

Who is thy father childe axt his mothers husband
Axe my mother (quoth he) that to vnderstand
The boy dalieth with you sir for verily
He knowth who is his father as well as I
The man of this childes wit was wrapt in such ioy
That he knew not what he might make of the boy

*   *   *   *   *

From these quotations the reader can form a fair idea of
the quality of the *Epigrammes*, but to appreciate them fully
he must read them all. This is not an onerous or unpleasant
task; there are so many epigrams and so many topics, so
diversely treated. They contain a rough, homely humour,
shrewd wit, and easy puns. It is not easy always to follow the
joke, and many of the conceits are to our ears tedious and far-
fetched. But I recommend them to the reader.

The *Epigrammes* will have more than one value for the
casual reader who will pick them and read them, appropriately
a few at a time, and haphazard. It would be unfair to them
and to their author to read them deliberately from end to end.
Many of them, no doubt, were thrown off on the spur of the
moment and fell very pat, especially when the wine had
circled.

At any rate, beside the 1562 and 1566 editions, other editions
appeared in 1567, 1587, and 1598. It is very likely that there
were even more editions, which, quite apart from the influence
it had on early biographers, who have always emphasized his
powers as an epigrammatist and conversationalist, goes to
prove the general popularity of this work.

I pray you readers to scan this
As I for mirth myrily did make it
So you in mirth myrily will take it

* * * * *

We may turn now to a little internal evidence from this work, which is undoubtedly Heywood's, (i) on the authorship of doubtful plays, (ii) on his life.

In Epigram 20 in "The Firste Hundred" we get the old Heywoodian collocation of "bable" and "fable":

Who heareth all
And all bableth
Whateuer fall
He ofte fableth

And in Epigram 98 of "The Fifth Hundred of Epygrams" there is a reference to "Frances Fabler."

In Epigram 66 of "The Fifth Hundred of Epygrams" there is a reference too that calls to mind "neighbour Prat" of the play:

Of what length is Iohn long the carier Prat

In Epigram 48 of the "Three Hundred" occurs for the *third time* the proverb we have first noted in *Johan,*

The paryshe priest forg[ett]eth he was paryshe clarke.

* * * * *

These slight references and the constant use of Alliteration, etc., corroborate a little more the ascription of the three plays to Heywood.

But the strongest corroboration, of course, comes from the famous Epigram 100:

Art thou Heywood that hath made *many mad plaies.*

There are three distinct references to university life, one in the epigram which has been quoted and the others in

Epigrams 55 and 56 of "The Fifth Hundred of Epygrams," which contain references to "Brodegates" (Pembroke) and "Brazennose."

    *   *   *   *   *

And so we come to the latest, the most novel, and most remarkable expression of Heywood's genius.

THE SPIDER AND THE FLIE

A parable of the Spider and the Flie made by
John Heywood
Imprinted at London in Flete Strete by
Tho. Powell
Anno 1556

THIS Parable was accurately reprinted (with an introduction) by A. W. Ward for the Spenser Society in 1894.

On the back of the elaborately engraved title-page is a wood-cut purporting to be a full-length portrait of John Heywood, and inscribed I. H. A man is shown in a flat cap with a long furred gown which critics have taken to be a university costume. The introspective profess to detect a certain sadness in his lineaments. At the top and bottom of the engraving are masks of Tragedy and Mirth. The engraving is repeated in the book.

The Parable is profusely illustrated with woodcuts which were much admired when they were made, and which are still entertaining, often astonishing, and never without merit.

*　　　*　　　*　　　*　　　*

The argument of the Parable is given in "The Table" at its beginning.

A Flie chanced to fall into a Spider's web. The Spider fell into "a dreadfull wonder" at the sudden shaking of his cobweb, "then taking comfort entreth in quarel with the flie," who asks to be allowed to speak and makes an oration on "justice and just justicers, requiring to have his cause heard throughlie and adjudged justlie."

They now "entre into the principal argument" and the

Spider chargeth the Flie with burglarie or with felonie or with trespas.

The Flie makes his defence against all three charges and they now fall into a discussion of custome; and the Flie "cleymeth all hooles in all windowes to be flies in freeholde."

"Whereon sueth a glaunce at the diuersite of gouernement after which they agree to refer the matter to arbiterment," the Spider and the Flie choosing respectively as arbiters the Ant and the Butterflie. The Ant and the Butterflie are briefed and prepare their arguments, taking the advice of a representative Spider and a representative Flie. Whereupon, after much discussion upon "credence woorship and honestie," they decide that both sides are equally credible and honest.

Now stand forth a "tart taunting spider" and "a sharpe saucie flie," "on tip toes to chop logike eche with other in rude reasoning of this case."

It is still stale-mate; and so "eche side among themselfes fall in mourmuring." "Whereat with twynke of an iye" the head Spider builds "a strong castell in the copweb with ordnaunce and weapons and spiders redie in order of defence," and "a huge heape of flies light aboute tharbiters and apprehend thant casting a halter about his necke drawing him to their Tree of Reformacion to hang him streyght."

The Ant, only after a brusque speech by the Butterflie, is allowed to speak in his defence, and by his defence sets the flies in fear of the spiders. The Ant is therefore spared and sent to the Spiders to set them in fear of the Flies. He only just fails, and when he returns to the Flies he narrowly escapes death again through a bold last-minute message to the Flies from the chief of the Spiders.

Now begins a furious onslaught by the Flies upon the stronghold of the Spiders, after which both sides want peace. Peace is concluded by the intercession of the Ant, who retires wiser and sadder to a molehill, where he is solemnly received by his wife and children. He declines to take any further part in the dispute and the Spiders and Flies distribute among themselves the holes in the windows.

Now the discussion between the chief Spider and the Flie in the web is resumed. The Flie appeals in turn to reason, law, custom, and conscience; but is compelled at the last to own himself beaten and to resign himself to death. He gives death-bed advice to his friends and is just about to be killed by the Spider when the Maid of the House "commeth in and striketh the copweb and the spider to the ground."

The Spider, in his turn, is now about to die and appeals in his turn to reason, law, custom, and conscience; but "in reasoning of both sides the maid driueth the spider to graunt himself conuinst." Whereupon the Maid "decreth the spider to die."

"After a few wofull woordes of the spider had to his sonne (they both claspynge eche other in armes verie naturally) he kysseth and blisseth him."

The Maid then presses the Spider to death with her foot and after a few words of advice about the harms of "mysorder" to the assembled Spiders and Flies, "she sweepyth the wyndow cleane in euerie place: which doone she departeth."

* * * * *

The maide being gone the auctor cumeth in. And upon hys beholding the wyndow fayre and cleane swept withoute anie combirous copweb or excessive flockes of flies he departeth.

* * * * *

The Parable is excessively long, and though never quite without interest it has had many harsh critics.

L. Harison in *Chronicles of Holinshed*, 1577, declares that it was so profound that, like the poetry of Browning, even its author failed to understand it. George Ellis, in his *Historical Sketch of English Poetry*, 1801, finds it utterly contemptible. Thomas Warton, in his *History of English Poetry*, 1824, mentions that it was never reprinted.

It is indeed a "large and laboured performance." But, as
A. W. Ward asks, who reads *through The Faerie Queene*? He
retorts that many of the critics have spoken without their
book and have rushed into literary criticism without reading
the allegory.

At the same time it cannot be denied fairly that much of it
is tedious, and that, though parts of it are excellent, e.g. the
light Chaucerian opening, much of the close argumentation,
all the action, particularly when the Ant is at the Tree of
Reformation, and again when the Flies make their grand
assault, nevertheless, the claim cannot be sustained that the
book is an artistic success. There are many intolerably long
and barren patches which none but the critics would peruse;
and which, like some of the plays, only have their interest
to-day because they are so dull.

*   *   *   *   *

The Parable as such must have a secondary meaning. But
what is this meaning?

It has been often said that the Spiders represent the Protestants and the Flies the Catholics. But the opposite view is
equally tenable.

From reading the Parable we may remember:—

(i) that the Spider has a wife and two children;

(ii) that the Flies outnumber the Spiders by twenty to
one;

(iii) that the Butterflie addresses the Spiders as "Masters,
or Lords, spiders";

(iv) that

Flies have ever had cause to mislike war most
When Spiders and Flies have fallen at this like jar
For quarrels wherein Flies might most their right boast
Whoever had right the Flies the field lost
To one score Spiders slain, Flies slain twenty score
And much of their offspring lost for evermore;

(v) that the Spiders did not begin the war and that the Flies are the invaders;

(vi) that "if Flies shall Spiders conquer Then are all Spiders lost," but "that kind of conquest . . . never was, nor is, nor never like to be";

(vii) that

> from the beginning
> When Flies against Spiders have thus rebelled
> They had miserable overthrow in rebelling;

(viii) that the Flie refutes the charge of Rebellion, and the Spider's claim that of those who die in this struggle "Spiders go to bliss quite and Flies to bale";

(ix) that an attack is delivered upon "neuter-like indifferency";

(x) that the army of the Flies is a motley medley;

(a) "tag and rag"; and
(b) "Seldom hath been seen such a sort and all so stout";
(c) "Except here and there one temperate to behold
  Staves bats clubs pitchforks most beggarly most bold";
(d) "The Flies are in number above the Spiders far" whereas
(e) "The Spiders in order far better than they" are provided with all sorts of ordnance, "handguns, hakes, arquebusses, culverins, cannons double and demy";
(f) "Each of them harnessed meet for his property
  The rest all in bright harness cap-a-pie";

(xi) that the Flies have "long spited the Spiders," "laying their fault on the back" of the Spiders, "claiming their commons and such other like and slandering their titles";

(xii) that in his dying oration the Flie admits that:

> Spiders are placed above superiorly
> And Flies beneath them placed inferiorly;

(xiii) that "the Maid of the House" prefers the trouble of the Flies to the trouble of the Spiders;

(xiv) that she felt convinced that it was her duty to kill the
      Spider;

It is true that the author calls it "a parable." But no other
parable has such an obscure second meaning, e.g. it is impossible to claim on these extracts that the Spiders represent
either Catholics or Protestants.

*   *   *   *   *

In the "Conclusion with an exposission of the auctor
touching one peece of the latter part of this *parable*" Heywood
says:

> I have good readers this parable pende
> After olde beginning newly brought to ende
> The thing yeres mo than twentie since it begoon
> To the thing yeres mo than ninetene nothing doon . . .
> Begon with the first and ended with the last

*   *   *   *   *

It was published in 1556. So we are carried back at least
till 1536. Now what were the events of this period most likely
to inspire Heywood?

(i) His friend and patron, Sir Thomas More, was executed
    in 1535, and impressed all Western Christendom by
    the tragedy of his death. Can any place be found for
    him among the protagonists of the Parable?

(ii) In 1536 the Pilgrimage of Grace was made as a protest
     against the Suppression of the Monasteries. Can it
     be that Heywood began his allegory hot with the
     inspiration of this awkward and dangerous effort by
     the masses to take authority into their own hands,
     an effort which for some time overbore all attempts
     to quell it; and that despite his sympathies with the
     movement he dared not to profess them? And was
     the grand captain of the Flies Robert Aske?

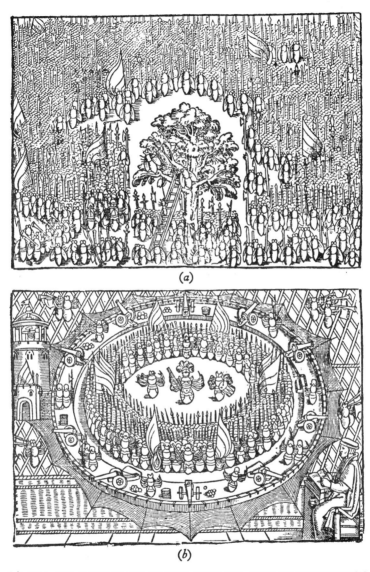

(a) THE ANT ABOUT TO BE HANGED FROM THE TREE OF REFORMATION
(b) THE COBWEB CASTLE

(iii) Heywood's own imprisonment and great personal danger for his share in the plot against Cranmer about 1539. After which he had to recant like the Ant, "with a halter about his neck."

(iv) The imprisonment of his father-in-law John Rastell—a Flie suffering at the hands of a Spider, Cranmer.

(v) Robert Ket's Rebellion. This broke out in 1549, and was due more to social, rather than to religious, discontent. The tanner administered justice under "the Oak of Reformation," which directly calls to mind "the Tree of Reformation" of the Flies.

This rising was suppressed by the Duke of Northumberland; was he the Head Spider, doomed to suffer in his turn?

The allegory certainly seems to dwell more upon *social* rather than religious evils of the day.

(vi) Wyatt's Rebellion. This was suppressed in 1554. There is much in the allegory about rebellion.

(vii) The martyrdom of his great religious opponent Cranmer. Was he the Head Spider who suffered at the hands of the Maid?

(viii) The execution of the Duke of Northumberland in 1553. He was the head of the Protestant plot against the succession of Mary. Is his death referred to in the crushing of the Head Spider under Mary's foot?

(ix) Mary's marriage with Philip in 1554, and the apparent restoration for ever of orthodox Catholicism.

These are the principal events that might have inspired the Parable.

*   *   *   *   *

If we turn again to the Conclusion we find Heywood says:

this figure here implies
For strife in windows between Spiders and Flies
The plat of all the world and he refers the reader particularly to Chapters 88 and 92 of the allegory.

In Chapter 88 in his dying speech the Flie advises twelve grave Flies not to contend with their "biggers," "to leave off strife and live by loss in rest" because "Spiders are placed above superiorly and flies beneath them inferiorly" and "law inhibiteth quite Flies to fight against their high heads," which might be an injunction that the proletariat are to accept their social and feudal lot.

In Chapter 92 in his dying speech the Spider says:

> When my winning was most I thought it too small
> The shooting at all was my mark principal

and

> good mistress maid
> Your displeasure toward me to bring appeased
> I pray your benignity to be displayed
> To forgive my guilt which hath you displeased
> And not only displeased but diseased

The Spider accuses himself of "subtlety," "wrong usurping," "pride," "wrath," and "hate." This might be an injunction against the arrogance of anyone.

*　　　*　　　*　　　*　　　*

Heywood also states in the Conclusion that the Maid who "took in hand to sweep her window his realm" is our sovereign lady Queen Mary, that her "master" is Christ and her "mistress" "mother holy Church Catholical."

> She thought her duty it being her charge
> To do some execution for *warning large*
> *Both to Spiders and Flies* the flocks every one
> By executing of Spiders only one
> And save custom of justice forced her thereto
> Loath was she execution on him to do

This last passage, perhaps written early in the reign of Mary, may refer to the burning of Cranmer or the execution of Northumberland.

*   *   *   *   *

But I feel it is impossible to distinguish Spider and Flie as Protestant and Catholic; or to see any partiality in Heywood's treatment of Spider or Flie.

Indeed, in the preface Heywood admits that *twenty useful* interpretations may be placed on one parable and advises his readers to apply any morals they can find to themselves; and no religious insinuation is made till half-way through the book. It seems the work is more a pamphlet on social evils reminiscent of William Langland.

In Chapter 7 the Flie makes an "oration commending justice and just justicers." The Spider replies with a lecture on Reason, Law, Custom, and Conscience; and later accuses the Flie of felony, burglary, and trespass, and so on. Many social evils of the day are discussed—of the jury system, of land tenure, of the laws of trespass, of corruption, of the grievances of landlords and tenants.

There are also many pages of discussion devoted to the different forms of government, the respective rights of landlords and tenants, and of different castes.

The first and almost the only reference to religion is in Chapter 44, when, after a long discussion of rents and prices, the Spider says to the Flie:

I durst lay my life thou art an heretic

a statement from the Spider which makes it difficult to suppose that by the Spider Heywood meant to represent Cranmer.

*   *   *   *   *

All interpretations therefore of the Parable will be made at hazard; and my conclusion after reading this allegory closely is that it reflects the social evils of the day and the points of difference between the upper and lower classes; and that Heywood was too much a man of the world, with too big a sense of proportion, not to be able to see both sides of a social or even of a religious question.

For these and many other reasons I regard this book as a useful commentary on social conditions in Heywood's day, written by him with little or no tractarian bias.

Perhaps when Heywood began the Parable he had certain grievances in view: the misfortunes of his father-in-law; his own misfortunes; the advance of the Protestant heresy; the dangerous power of Cranmer, who turned the Commission of Catholics against him, and into a Commission of Cranmer against Catholics.

But the fate which overtakes all books begun at one period of a man's life and concluded twenty years later, has overtaken this book. He had had to adapt an old book in the light of the experience of twenty years. The result is that he constantly shifts his ground and mystifies his readers deliberately or accidentally just when they are apparently on a hot scent.

The poem appears to have begun as a political, social, or religious pamphlet. It ended as a laudatory poem on Queen Mary; and to-day it is impossible to distinguish the verses and the views of 1536 when they have been coloured or enlarged or modified by the experience of later life.[1]

[1] One notices in the Parable:

    (i) the Debate—the "Mastery"—and Logic Chopping—with all the logical terminology of the day and the usual Recapitulation;

    (ii) the constant use of Proverbs, Alliteration, and Cumulation of words in sentences and the beginning of many consecutive verses with the same word;

    (iii) the Introduction, which clearly shows the influence of Chaucer, from whom Heywood has borrowed freely in his plays;

    (iv) the Alliteration of the *dramatis personae*—Margaret, Marion, and Margery; and of Pierce Pismore and Bartlemy Butterfly;

    (v) the recurrence of the name Margery;

    (vi) The conclusion of the allegory on a *moralizing* note.

TEXT OF FOUR PLAYS

In the following pages is given a faithful text of four of Heywood's plays. The best way to understand a man is to meet him face to face. The next best thing is to read his books. I commend these four plays to the reader, and of the four I commend particularly the last three. They have an intrinsic modern interest. They have also the interest of the curio and the article of vertu.

A PLAY OF
WYTTY AND WYTTLES

FROM THE ORIGINAL MANUSCRIPT IN THE BRITISH MUSEUM:
HARLEIAN MS. 367

I

[A PLAY OF WYTTY AND WYTTLES]

*   *   *   *   *

JOHN

A mervelus mater marcyfull lord
Yf reason whyth this conclewsyon acord
better to be a folle than a wyse man

JAMES

Better or wurs I seay as I began
Better ys for man that may be wyttles
Then wytty

JOHN

Ye show some wytty wyttines

JAMES

Experyens schall wyttnes my tale trewe
And for temperall welth let vs fyrst vewe
And that experyens may schowe the trewer
Accept we reson to be owr wewer
In wh[ich] reson by experyens we knowe
That folk most wytty to whom ther doth growe
By frendds dedd befor nowght left them be hynde
Nor by lyvyng frendds no lyvyng a snyde
Except they wyll storve ther fyndyng must they fynd
By muche payne of body or more payne of mynde
And as for the wyttles as who saythe the sott
The naturall foole cald or thydeot
From all kynds of labor that do the payne constrayne
As farr as suffycyency nedythe obtayne
In sewrty of lyvyng the sot doth remayne

JOHN

In sewrty of lyvyng but not w[ith]owt payne
For admyte all sotts in case as be mayny
That leve w[ith]owt labor yet wher ys any
But for that one plesewr he hathe mor payne
Then the wytty wurker in all dothe sustayne
What wretch so faryth payne havyn eny wytt
Lyke the wyttles wretche none yf ye mark hyt
Who cumeth by the sott who cumeth he by
That vexythe hym not somewey usewally
Some beat hym some bob hym
Some joll hym some job hym
Some tugg hym by the hers
Some lugg hym by the eares
Some spet at hym some spurne hym
Some toss hym some turne hym
Some snap hym some scratch hym
Some cramp hym some cratch hym
Some cuff [hym] some clowt hym
Some lashe hym some lowte hym
Some whyske hym some whype hym
Wythe scharpe naylys some nype hym
Not evyn mayster somer the kyngs g[r]acys foole
But tastythe some tyme some nyps of new schoole
And by syd thys kynde of frettyng and fewmyng
Another kynd of turment in consewmyng
The wytty to the wyttles oft invent
After inventyon of yer full entent
The foole by flatery to turment ys browght
So farr overjoyd and his brayne so wyde wrowght
That by joy of a jewell skant wurth a myght
The sott oft slepyth no wynk in a whole nyght
And for ensampyll wyth a walsyngam ryng
Thys dystemperans to the sot ye may bryng

And mak hym joy theryn as hyt war a thyng
Or prys to peyse the rawnsome of a kyng
In joying whereof yf any man got way
To get yt from hyn as every chyld may
Then man & chyld seth the sot in such case
That nowght but paynfull sorow takyth any place
By thys small proses a small wytt may ges
That wyd wer the wytty to wysh them wyttles

JAMES

Theffect of this yowr matter as ye spak yt
Standythe much yn two poynts as I tak yt
Of whyche tweyne the tone ys that the sot hath
By jollyng and jobbyng and other lyk skath
Extreame payne wyth extremyte of yer
Thother ys after frettyng fewryus fyer
That the foole w[ith] eche frewtles tryflyng toy
Is so dystempryd w[ith] dystemperat joy
That as much payne brynght his pleasaunt passyon
As dothe the pynchyng of his most paynfull fassyon
These two poynts consyderyd the sot as ye say
Hathe some payne sometyme but most tymes I say nay

JOHN

Then from no payne to some payne the wyttles are browght

JAMES

Ye but wytty and wyttles wyttly wrowght
By some payne to suche payne that wytty fele most
Then wytty and wyttles eche part his part bost
Tak of wytty the degres and nomber all
And of yt nombyr I thynke ye nōbyr small
But that eche one of them ys of nede asynd
To labor sore yn body or ells yn mynde
And few to all that fortewne so doth favor
But yn body & mynde bothe they do labor

And of body thes labors the most paynefullest
Is the labor of mynde I have hard gest
And lest bothe paynes or most of twayne be to
    towght
For yow to matche w[ith] and the lest payne inowgh
To the fyrst most payne of ye wyttles nody
Joyne we the wyttyse least payne payne of body
Who seth what payne labor bodyly bryngth
Schall easely se thereby how the body wryngth
Husband mens plowyng or earyng and sowyng
Hedgyng and dychyng w[ith] repyng and mowyng
In cartyng such lyftyng such burdenns bareyng
That payne of the body bryngth these to stareyng
And muche of thys done yn tyme of such het
That yn colde cave covryd the carcas must swet
Some other use crafts in wh[ich] wurck ys so small
That yn somer plesaunttly they lyve all
Who in wynter when husbondmen warme w[ith] wark
In that they may not sturr for cold or evyn stark
Some yn wynter fryse some yn somer fry
And the wyttles do the nother for comenly
Other whythe wurshypfull or honorabull
He temprately standith in howse at the tabyll
And of all his labors rekyn the hole rabyll
Bygger burden barth he none then his babyll
So that from thes paynes or th[e] lyk recytyd
The wyttles hath warrant to be aquyghtyd
And sewr the sotts pleasewre in this last aquyghtall
Cownterwaylth his payne in yowr fyrst recyghtall
For vnto the sotts nyppyng and beatyng
Joyne the wytty laborers nypps and freatyng
And whether ye cownt by yer month or weke
Ye shall fynde thease of the wytty to seek
As far as of the wyttles and of bothe sorts
This ys the dyfferens that to me ymports

Sotts are coyld of other the wytty coylth hymself
What choyse thus alegyd

JOHN

Small ah horson elf
Somewhat he towchyth me now yn very deed
Howbeyt to thys am not I yet full agred
The wytty who beate them selves by bysynes
May oft yn beatyngs favowr them selves I ges
Such oportewnyte by wytt ye ofte espyd
That labor by wytt ys ofte qualyfyd
In takyng tyme or place as best may stand
Most easely to dyspatch things cumyng in hand
Wytt hathe provytyon alway for releef
To provyd some remedy agaynst myscheef
Wytty tak bysynes as wytty wyll mak yt
And as wytty beat wyttles must tak yt

JAMES

Tak yt howe ye lyst ye can mak yt no les
But wytty have suche payne as my worde wyttnes
ffor thowgh wytt for tyme sometyme may payne prevent
Yet yn most tymes theyr foreseyd payne ys present
Whyche payne in the wytty wyttyly weyde
May match payne of the wyttles by ye fyrst leyd
And to the second poynt for dystemporat joyes
By havyng or hopyng of fancyes or toyes
In wyttles or wytty bothe tak I as one
ffor thowgh the thyngs that wytty have or hope on
Are yn some kynd of acownt thyngs muche gretter
Then thyngs of the sotts joyings yet no whyt better
Nor les payne bryngth yt passhyon but endyferent
To bothe except wytty have the woors turment
Thynk yow aright good wytty havyng clerely
A thowsand pownd sodaynly gyven hym yerely

Who befor that owre myght dyspend no peny
Nor tyll that owre never lokyd for eny
Myght not joy as much yt soden recevyng
As joyth the sott reseyte of hys walsyngam ryng
And therby be kepte from quyet sleepe a wek
As well as the ryng maketh the sotte sleep to seek
And in a soden leesyng that gyfte agayne
Myght not the wytty be presyd w[ith] payne
As depe as the wyttles his ring stolne or lost
And thowgh thys ensampyll chanse seeld when at most
Yet sometyme yt happyth and dayly we see
That folk far from wyttles passhynyd be
By joyfull hope of thyngs to them lyk to hape
Or havyng of thyngs plesaunt lat lyght in the lap
As muche to theyr vnrest for dystemprancy
As ye showde the wyttles restles formerly
And oft tyme for cawse consydryd and weyd
As lyght as yowr walsyngam ryng aforseyd
Wytt in wytty hathe seelyd such perfecshyon
To bryng dysposyshyn full in abieckshyon
And the dyphers of dysposhshyon ys such
Some wytts hope to lyttyll some wytts hope to much
By whyche over much I sey and sey must ye
That wytty and wyttles one in thys case be
And thus in both casys rasonyng cawse showth
Cawse to conclewd that to the wytty growth
As muche payne as to the wyttles wherby
As good be wyttles as wytty say I

JOHN

That conclewsyon ys conclewdyd wysely
Your pryme proposycyon dyd put presysely
Better to be wyttles then wytty and now
As good to be wyttles as wytty sey yow

But that wytt whych putth case in degre cōparatyve
And conclewdyth case in degre posytyve
Sall not in that case clame degre sewperlatyve

JAMES

Ye pas in this tawnt yowr prerogatyve
But that wytt whych bostythe ye full of his wynnyng
As thowghf ke knewe thend of thing at begynnyng
That wytt schall schow wyttles ympedymēt
To be takyn wytty w[ith] wytts exelent
I conclewd her not for thend but for the myds
Whyche yf ye will her to end as reason byds
Ye schall perceyve and also condysend
To grawnt me thanks then yn that I entende
Yowr fall by fear handelyng to be ye mor fayr
To set ye downe featly stayer after stayer
And so by a fayer fygewre of ynducksyn
To bryng y[our] parte softe and fayer to distrucksshyn
ffor wher ye grawnt fully for owght your worde make
That as much payne wytty as wyttles doth take
So from thys myds to the end I schall prowe
That most payne of twayne to the wyttles doth move
For as I lode egally paynes of body
To wytty and wyttles lyke wyse wyll I
Over lode the wytty w[ith] payne of mynde
In mater as playne as can be asynde
Whyche payne of mynde in mete mesewr to wey
Ys mor paynfull then payne of body I sey

JOHN

Ye sey so and seyd so but so seyd not I
Nor sey yt not yet but that seyng deny
And tyll sayng prove y[our] sayng more playnely
I wyll asay to sey the contrary

I thynk paynes of body cowntyd in ech kynde
May compare w[ith] all kynde of paynes of mynde

JAMES

Yf ye assewrydly thynk as ye sey now
I thynk ye thynk as few men thynk but yow
Howbeyt that beyng but an ynsydent
To pryncypall purpose presently ment
Yet that excepshyn took yow wyttyly
For had ye grawntyd that as ye schall schortly
Then forthw[it]h shold owr pryncypall proses
Have concludyd in the part that I profes
For a meane whervnto as mesewr may
Meet vnmesewrabull thyng as who say
Joyne in lyke proporshyn as may be ment
The meane laborer to the meane studyent
And ye schall anon fynd the stewdyents payne
More paynfull then the laborers labor playne

JOHN

The stewdyents payne ys oft plesantly myxt
In felyng what frewt by his study ys fyxt

JAMES

The laborers labor qu̇yghtth that at a whypp
In felynge the frewt [of] hys wurkmanshyp
As muche delyght carters oft in carts neat trymd
As do studyents yn bokes wythe golde neate lymd
And as much envy who may dreve hys cart best
As among stewdyents who may seme lernd hyest
Wherby inwarde delyght to tolle forthe eche part
Semthe me yndyfrent to art or to cart
And furder meane labor in most comon wyse
Ys most parte hansome and holsome excersyse
That purgyth hewmors to mans lyfe and quycknes

Whyche study bredyth to mans dethe or sycknes
Also most kynds of labor most comenly
Strane most grose owtewarde partes of the body
Wher study sparyng sholders fyngers and tose
To the hedd and hart dyrectly study gose
Pervert ys your jugment yf ye iudge not playne
That less ys the parell and les ys the payne
The knockyng of knockylls whyche fyngers dothe strayne
Then dyggyng yn the hart or drying of the brayne

JOHN

For comun meane kynde in bothe parts now leyde
I see not but reason saythe as ye have seyde

JAMES

The labor of body and mynde thus compare
In what degrese ye can devyse to declar
Betwene bothe beyng not kynt yn suche degre
But that thone from thother seperate may be
And that bothe labors yn joynyng ye arecte
As lyke yn degre as wytt may coniecte
And bothe ons ser[c]hyd ser[c]he schall mak warantyse
In labor of mynde the wurst payne doth aryse

JOHN

Methynketh I cowld mak yt other wyse apere
Save I lack tyme to dylate matter her
For tyme of reasonyng wold be long therin
And tyme of reasonyng must be short here in
Whyche weyd w[ith] that this standeth but insydently
To owr present porpose pryncypally
I grawnt to agree as ye have defynd
Of labor of body and labor of mynde
That labor or payne of mynd ys the greter
And thys now grawntyd what be ye the better

JAMES

So muche the bettyr and yow so muche the wurs
That ye may now put your toong in your purs
For any woord in defens yowr toong shall tell
After these my next woords gyve ear and mark well
This labor of myndd whyche we now agre
Above labor of body we must decre
To joyne sole to the wytty for possybly
Cannot the wyttles tak part of that payne

JOHN

Why

JAMES

How can he have payne by imagynacyon
That lackythe all kynds of consyderatyon
And yn all sencys ys so ynsofycyent
That nowght can he thynk in owght t[hat] may be ment
By any meane to devyn ony self thing
Nor devyse in thyng past present or cumyng
No more hathe he in mynde other payne or car
Then hathe other cock my hors or Iyll my mar
Thys cawse w[ith] wyttles payne of mynde dyspensys
But the wytty havyng all vytall sensys
Hathe therby and ynwarde clock whyche mark who wyll
May oftymes go false but yt never standyth styll
The plummets of that clock come never to grownde
Imagynatyon ys watche and gothe so rownd
To whyche consyderacyon gyvyth so quyck ear
That in the wytty mynd the restles rest ys ther
A small wytt may ges no wone wytt can deme
How many or how myche ar theyr paynes extreme
Nor how many contrary kyndes in some one brest
If ye perceyve thys tale ye se yt wytnest
Thre thyngs of wyche the fyrst ys that the wyttles

Off labor or payne of mynde have reles
The second ys that the wytty have in ûre
All paynes of mynde and that wytty doth yt procur
Thyrdly I glanset at payne of mynd allewdyng
That payne to be most payne   As in for conclewdyng
Perceyve ye this

JOHN

Ye and grawnt yt trew to

JAMES

Then must ye grawnt wytty to have most payne

JOHN

So I do

JAMES

If wytty have most payne of tweyne ye must say
Better to be wyttles than wytty

JOHN

Nay

JAMES

I say yes

JOHN

I say nay and wyll so envey
That I wyll hold ye wagg a nother way
As I grawnt wytty of twayne most payne endewr
So wyll I prove wytty to have most plesewr
Whych plesewer shall bothe drowne the wyttyse payne
And the plesewer yn whyche the wyttles remayne

JAMES

Thys p[ro]myse wyll hardly bryng good paymēt
Fot yt ys a strange kynde of argewmēt
To p[ro]ve hym in most plesewre who hath most payne
Or hym yn least payne who least plesewre doth sustayne

JOHN

Let vs reason all plesewrs on both sydes
And then let that syde have best that best provydes

JAMES

All pleswrs on bothe sydes that wer a thyng
To make vs make ende to morow mornӯg

JOHN

As now the best parte of my parte cumth on
Ye make marvelus hast ye wold fayne be gone

JAMES

Right now yowr self cowld wey in right wytty sort
That resonyng her now of reason must be short

JOHN

Yt schal be short ynowgh yf ye tak awey
All that parte that for my part effeckt dothe ley

JAMES

I wyll nother tak awey all nor tak all
But for a meane betwene bothe my selfe streyght schall
Alege not plesewrs all I sey but such one
As over weythe other plesewrs evry chone
Whych plesewre wher yt in fyne dothe not remayne
All plesewrs in all parts ar plesewrs but vayne
Of whyche one plesewre the wyttles ar sewre evyr
And of that plesewre wytty ar sewr nevyr

JOHN

What plesewr ys that

JAMES

Plesewr of salvashyon
I thynk yowr self wyll affyrme affyrmashyon
That from owre forfathers syn orygynall
Bapty[s]m sealyth vs all a quyttās generall
And faythe of ynfants whyle they infants abyde
In faythe of parents for the churche ys supplyd
Wherby tyll wytt take root of dysernyng
And betweene good a[nd] yll geve perfyght warnyng
Wherever innosents innosensy dyspewt
For thowghts worddes or dedes god doth none yll ympewt
Where god gyvyth no dyscernyng god taketh none acownte
In whyche case of acownt the sot dothe amownt
ffor no more dysernythe the sott at yeres thre score
Then thynosent borne w[ith] in yeres thre before
This short saynge yf ye yn mynde revolve
Then schall thys long debate forthw[ith] dysolve

JOHN

Syr I graunt sotts shall be saved as ye tell
And safe shall wytty be to yf they do well

JAMES

Yff they do well   that yf altryth much lo
Theffeckte of my sentens to wyttles

JOHN

How so

JAMES

That yf leyd for the wytty purportth a dowte
But all dowtes in the wyttles ar scrapt clene owt

I

Sans dowte the wyttles ys sewer of salvashyon
Wherby I to conclewde thys communycashyon
Make wytty sewer of all plesewrs can be leyde
Dowtyng lack of none but thys one plesewer last seyde
And of all plesewrs wyttless to have none
Savyng he standth in sewrte of this one
Ys not the sewrte of thys one much bettyr
Then of the rest thowgh the nomber be grettyr

JOHN

Yes

JAMES

Lyk as a goose can say nothyng but hys
So hath he now nothyng nothing to say but yes
And in affyrmyng my sayng he sayth thys
In whyche he grawntth hys partt not partly a mys
But all a mys as who seythe in all placys
The sum whereof in bothe partes standth in thre casys
Off wh[ich] thre thargewment of the fyrst was thus
In laboryus payne of body to dyscus
Who soferythe more the wytty or the sott
Yn whyche by bothe assents we knyt thys knott
That as muche payne of body in effeckte hathe ye one
As thother conclewdyng thus ffar thervppon
As good to be wyttles as wytty and then
We argewde labor or payne of mynd in men
Wherin I dryvyng hym to grawnt payne of mynde
More then payne or labor bodyly defynd
In the second case I payne of mynde provyng
To wytty and not to wyttles to be movyng
Drave hym to grawnt furder that by t[hat] payne
Better w[ith]owte wytt then w[ith] wytt to remayne
Now in this thyrd case wher ye mad a bragg
By plesewrs in the wytty to hold me wagg

And plesewrs of the wyttles to overwhelme
I stamyng in w[ith] hym stack so to the helme
That hys parte fynally to shypwrack ys browght
The sewrte of all plesewrs in this world wrowght
Match not the sewrte of plesewr eternall
And the state of sotts have none acownt so carnall
That god ympewtetthe any yll to them I say
And the wyttyse acownt awgmentth evry day
And thawdytors wytt who schall tak thacownt so cler
He forgeth not wone worde in a thowsand yer
What ned mo woords I thynk the least wytt her
Sethe thes thre casys on my syd so aper
That in the two fyrst casys temporally
And in this thyrd and last case spyrytewall
Ys sene fully I may conclewde fynally
Better to be wyttles then to be wytty

JOHN

So sey I now to by owr blyssyd lady
I gyve vpp my part and y[our] part playnly
Off wytty and wyttles I wyshe now rather
That my chyld may have a fool to hys father
The pyth of yowr conclewsyons be all so pewr
That better be a foole then a wyse man sewr

JEROME

Not so althowgh yowr fancy do so surmyse
Not better for man to be wytles then wyse
Nor so good to be wyttles as wytty nother
Thus ys yowr wytt dysseyved in other

JOHN

Why what dyffrens betwene wyse and wytty

JEROME

As muche sometyme as betwene wysdom and folly

JOHN

Man can in no wys be wys w[ith]owt wytt

JEROME

No and man may have gret wytt and wysdom nowght
Wytt ys the wurker of all perseyvyng
And indyfert to good or yll wurkyng
And as muche wytt may be in thyngs of most yll
As in the best thyngs wytt can aspyr vntyll
In vertu or vys I meane and wytt hath receyght
Off non yll where vppon wysdom doth weyght
Wysdome governth wytt alwey vertu to vse
And all kynds of vys alway to refewse
Thus ys wysdom in good part takyn alweyse
And gydythe wytt in all thyngs beyng thyngs of preyse
Thus thowgh ye must (as ye nede not) graunt his grownd
Whyche ys better wyttles then wytty to be fownd
Yet as muche as wysdom above wytt showth
So muche grawntyd ye hym more then of nede growthe

JAMES

Thys ys some yowng schooleman a fresh comonar
Hard ye the pryncypall that plantyd thys jar

JEROME

I hard all .

JAMES

And dothe not all on my syde fall

JEROME

No if ye had resonyd as I shall

JAMES

If ye as ye say have hard all he sayd
And yt is that saying have so widely wayd

To way my parte wurst herein in conclewsyon
Then ar ye wyttles yt we towe talkt on
But babyll y[ou]r will thys wyll I byd vppon
Better be sott somer then sage salamon

JEROME

Geve ye sentens or ye her what I cane say
Loo how wyll carythe hym and hys wytt away

JOHN

Syr yf ye hard all in my parte how say ye
What dyd I graunt hym to farr show I p[ra]y ye

JEROME

All that ye grauntyd welnye

JOHN

Nay I trow

JEROME

Ye shall when we have done not trow but know
For entre whereto I p[ra]y ye answer me
A questyon or twayne or mo yf nede be
And fyrst vnto thys answer as ye can
Whether wold ye be a resonable man
Or an vnresonabyll beast

JOHN

By and sell
I wolde be the symplest man betwene hevyn and hell
Rather than the best beast t¹ ever was bred

JEROME

Then yf ye of one of the twayne must be sped
Ye wolde be a maltman ye a myller
Rather then a mylhorse

¹ = yt.

JOHN

Be ye my well wyller

JEROME

Ye

JOHN

Spek no more of thys then what man fye
I wold not be a beast for all this world I
Wer yt for nowght ells but for this lyfe pr[e]s[n]t

JEROME

The tyme of thys lyfe in dede I meane and ment
But tell me why by yo[u]r faythe evyn playnely
Ye wyl not chang estate w[ith] the myll horse

JOHN

Why ther be whyse and wherforse I thyngk a thowsand
In cownt of two kynds of things cumyng in hande
Sensybyll plesewre and sensybyll payne
And fyrst for payne sustaynyd in thes twayne
Begyn w[ith] the myll hors whom ye put for prefe
Or any lyk beast sustaynyg the lyk grefe
And or I wold tak the payne the poore beests tak
I wolde eche day be twygd and tyd to a stak
Caryng fro the mill caryng to the myll
Drawyng in the myll poor jade he jetth styll
Ambyll he trot he go he a foot pase
Walop he galop he rack he in trase
Yf hys pase please not be yt softe or faster
The spurrs or whypp shal be hys pay master
Were not a man trow ye in plesaunt case
W[ith] a beast in thys case to change case or plase
No man except some few so ynfortewnate
That they be owt of thacownt of mans estat

That wolde agre to leve to chang paynes I trow
Wythe beasts payne beyng such as all men know
Now to spek of plesewr in thes twayne asynde
The beasts to cōpare ys to far behynde
Plesewr dyscussybyll in thes thus doth fall
The beast in effect hathe none the man hathe all
The resonabyll manns imagynashyon
Joynd w[ith] resonabyll consyderatyon
Bryngth man muche plesewr in consyderȳg
The plesant proporte of eche plesaunt thyng
Possesyd to mans behof at cōandyng
Beasts have thyngs of nede but no furder pleasyng
Syns man hathe releef for all nesessyte
As well as beaste and above beast cōmodyte
Of plesewrs plantyd for mans recreatyon
In the hyest kynd of mans contentatyon
Wherby plesewre in effect betwene thes twayne
Showth thus man hath all 'beast hathe none & more payne
Hathe beast then resonabyll man by thes bothe
Change fro man to beast who wyll I wolde be lothe

JEROME

Ye have yn my mynd thys right well defynde
And for cawse kepe yt well a while yn yowr mynde
Set we asyde man and beasts symylytewde
And full dysposytyon in bothe se we vewde
What thyng dysposythe most the varyet
Betwene man and beast

JOHN

Reson in ma(n)y perde

JEROME

That man who of reason ys as destytute
As a beast ys what dyffrens schall we dyspewte

JOHN

Small in this case excepte yt be this one
The sott hathe a resonabyll sowle beasts have none

JEROME

What helpyth ye wytt of the sowle in the sott
Syns the body ys suche yt vsythe yt not
Wher ympotensy plantth such ympedyments
That vse of sensys are voyd to all yntents
For vse of reason so that for vse of wytt
They ar as beasts wyttles vsyng wytt nowght
In man thus wyttles and thunreasonabyll beaste
I se small dyffrens for thys lyf at leaste

JOHN

I grawnt the wyttles and the beast thus as one

JEROME

Then shall thes beasts wyttles man and mylhors draw on
Bothe yn one yok for thynk yow the nombere
Standth as somer dothe all day yn slomber
Nay somer ys a sot foole for a kyng
But sots in many other mens howsyng
Bear water bear woodd and do yn drugery
In kychyn cole howse & in the nersery
And dayly for fawtes whych they cannot refrayne
Evyn lyke the myll hors they be whyppyd amayne
Other fooles that labor not have other conseyts
Vppon thydyll foole the flok ever mor weytes
They tos hym they turne hym he is jobd & jolde
Whyth frettyng and fewmyng as ye afore told
Except mayster somer of sotts not the best
But the myll hors may compar w[ith] hym for rest
Th[er]fore plesewr conceyvyng or receyvyng
The wyttles and mylhors are both as one thyng

Yowr last tale and thys tale together conferd
By matter of bothe let y[our] answer be hard
Whether ye wold be a man resonabyll
Or vnresonabyll and except ye fabyll
Thys answer shall show playne and vndowtydly
Whether ye wold be wyttles or wytty

JOHN

In good faythe I tak thys conclewcyon so full
That I may geve over and evyn so I wull
For thys lyf

JEROME

Well then for the lyf to come
Few woords wher rason ys may knyt vpp the sum
Concernyng plesewr after thys lyf present
By whych he and yow dyssolvyd argewment
Bothe parts by bothe partyse wer so endyd
That y[ou] part full fayntly ye defendyd
Thowgh the more meryt of owr redemptyon
Stande in crystys passyon yet in execusyon
Thereof shall we stand by gods justys except
Havyng tyme and wytt hys cōmandments be kepte
And who in whyche dothe most dylygently
Plant ymps of good woorcks gyvyn by god chefely
Most hyly of god shall he have rewarde

JOHN

How prove ye that

JEROME

By scryptur have in regard
Cryst in the gospell of John doth thys declar
In the howse of my father sayth crist ther are
Dyvers and many mantyons that ys to say
As thexposytyon of saynt Awstyne dothe way

There are in hevyn dyvers degrees of glory
To be receyved of men acordyngly
Eche man as he vsythe gods gyfts of grace
So schall he have in hevyn hys degre or place
But mark thys chefe grownd the sum of scrypture saythe
We must walk w[ith] these gyfts in the path of fayth
In whyche walk who wurkthe most in gods cōmandment
He shall have most & seynt powle showth lyk entent
As one starr dyfferthe from another in shynyng
So the resurectyon of the ded whych lyk thynge
Aperthe in other placys of scrypture

JOHN

I grawnt [thys] and what than

JEROME

That what cummth streyght in vre
Syns he that vsythe gods gyfts best schall have best
And he next who dothe next and so forth the rest
And that the wytty do dayly wurk or may
And the wyttles nowght wurkyth by no way
So that hys rewarde may cōpare in degre
If wytty have thys avantage thynkythe me
The wyse wyttyse place wyshe I desyrnfly
Rather then place of the wyttles

JOHN

So do I
Iff wyshe wolde wyn yt but where the sot ys sewr
The wytty standthe in hasardous adventewr
To lees all and so in fyne fayr and well
In sted of way to hevyn to tak the waye to hell
In wurks cōmandyd in faythe walkthe not
By gods justyce he hathe damnatyon in lott

And what other folkes fele I can not tell
But suche frayle falls fele I in my selfe to dwell
And by them to lees hevyn I am so adrad
The sotts sewrte of least joy ther wold I hadd
An old proverb makyth w[ith] thys whyche I tak good
Better one byrd in hand then ten in the wood

JEROME

What yf of the ten byrds in the wood eche one
Wer as good as that one in y[ou]r hand alone
And that ye myght cache them all ten yf ye wold
Wolde ye not leve one byrd for the ten now told

JOHN

Yes

JEROME

Wolde ye not havyng helpe tak resonabyll payne
For thonors of ten byrds for one in gayne

JOHN

Yes

JEROME

Then in gods name fear not let fle thys one
Ye schall I trust catche thes ten byrds evry chone
Your fleshly frayle falls ar suche yt ye drede
As muche as hope in havyng hevynly mede
By whych dred sewrte of joyes there ye most small
Wyshe ye rather then byd ventur to have joyes all
And th[e] soner by this ye chose thys I deme
The least joy there ys more then man can esteme
But now to remove thys block y[ou]r grett drede
We have a lever that removethe dred w[ith] spede
God sofrethe but not wylth ony man to syne
Nor god wylth no synners dethe but he be yn

Suche endless males yt his fynall estat
In lack of penytens mak hym selfe reprobate
In tyme of this lyf at eche penytent call
Owr marcyfull maker remytth synns all
From the perpetewall peyne infernall
Whatever they be from least to most carnall
By whyche goodnes of god we ar set in hopes chayer
Not to brede presumpsyon but to banysh despayr
The grace of god alwey to grace alewrthe man
And when man wyll call for gr[ac]e of gr[a]c[e] asewrth man
To assyst man gods cōmandments to fulfyll
At all tymes yf man cast owte yll wyllyng wyll
Howe syns the crystyane that wurkyth most in faythe
Schall have most in rewarde as the scrypture saythe
And t[hat] gods gr[ace] by gr[ace] cald for wyll asyst
Mans wyll to wurk well alwey when man lyst
And at instant of dew ordyrd penytens
Man hathe gods mercy of all former offens
Whyche showthe for mercy man ys not mor gredy
To ax then god to grawnt mercy ys redy
Thys sene what show yow to mayntayne the feare
Whyche ye toward desperatyon were in whyl [h]ear

JOHN

What show I   nay the show of that feare ys extyngkt
Evyn by thys praty tale thus pythyly lynkt
Syns god to the most faythfull wurker gyvyth most
And to mak man wurk muche god hasth as in post
And when man hath now wrowght at contrycyon
God grawnthe man of damnatyon remycyon
Makyng man sewre of frewte of crystys passyon
Except mans wylfull wyll mar all good fascyon
By this I dred god as standth w[ith] love & hope
But no desperate dred dothe my hart now grope

JEROME

Ten byrds in the wood or one in hand alone
Whych chos ye now

JOHN

I wyll not change ten for one
Syns the byrder wyl helpe me to tak them all
As sewr to myne vse as the one byrd cowld fall

JEROME

Well for conclewsyon syns ye sowndly se
That wytty have plesewr here in more degre
Then wyttles and also wytty wyse se ye
In hevyn by scrypture in hyer joyes be
Then the wyttles yow seyng thys clerly
Whether wold ye now be wyttles or wytty

JOHN

Wytty and the more wytty am I for you
Of which hartyly I thank yow and now
Where my mate my lords sayd that ys gone
Better be sot somer then sage salamon
In forsakyng that I woold now rather be
Sage saloman then sot somer I assewr ye

JEROME

As ye show wytt in change of former mynde
Beyng now from wytles to wytty enclynde
So aply y[ou]r wytt in what wytt schall devyse
As in good vse of wytt by grace ye may ryse
To be bothe wytty and wyttyly wyse
In governās of gods gyfts in suche syse
As wysdom alwey gydyth wherby thys schall fall
 Gods gyfts to gods glory bothe ye may vse and schall

Thes woords of cowncell in whych I now wadyd
   To hym whom I told them I onely osyne
I am by all cyrcumstance full perswadyd
   This sort beyng sortyd in sort thus fyne
   Nede none exortatyon or at least not myne
Thys sort have not onely by natewre hys wytt
But also by grace lyk wysdom joyned to yt

                 Thes thre stave next folowyng in
                   the kyngs absens ar voyde

And as in them therby gods gyfts shyne most may
   So stand ther affayres wherby they so shyne shall
If the glos of gods shyne not bryght eche way
   In them who havyng a realme in governall
   Set forthe theyr governans to gods glory all
Charytably aydyng subiects in eche kynde
The shynyng of gods gyfts wher shall we then fynde

And of this hye sort the hy hed most exelēt
   Ys owr most loved and drade supreme soferayne
The shynyng of whose most excellent talent
   Imployde to gods glory above all the trayne
   Thus wytt wantyth her recytall to retayne
And that all hys faythfull fele ye frewte of hys fame
Of corse I pray pardon in passyng the same

Praying that pryns whome owr pryns hys grete grace gave
   To grawnt hym long lenght of encres in estate
At full fyne wherof hys most hy gyfts to have
   By his most faythfull vse reward in suche rate
   As ys promysyd in scryptur alegyd late
The joyes not all onely inestymabyll
But more the degre of joyes incomparabyll

Contynewans wherof w[ith] frewtfull encrese
   I hartyly wyshe for encrese of rewarde
As scryptur alegyd late doth wytnes
   The wytty wyse wurker to be prefarde
Above thydyll sot and ye to regard
Eche man hym self so to aply in thys
As ye all may obtayne the hye degre of blys
                    Amen q[uo]d   John Heywod

THE PARDONER AND THE FRERE

FROM THE 1533 EDITION IN THE LIBRARY OF
MAGDALENE COLLEGE, CAMBRIDGE;

ONE OTHER COPY IS KNOWN.
NO OTHER EDITION IS KNOWN.

K

THE PARDONER AND THE FRERE

A MERY PLAY BETWENE

the pardoner and the frere, the curate
and neybour Pratte

Deus hic the holy trynyte
Preserue all that nowe here be
Dere bretherne yf ye wyll consyder
The cause why I am come hyder
Ye wolde be glad to knowe my intent
For I com not hyther for monye nor for rent
I com not hyther for meate nor for meale
But I com hyther for your soules heale
I com not hyther to poll nor to shaue
I com not hyther to begge nor to craue
I com not hyther to glose nor to flatter
I com not hyther to bable nor to clatter
I com not hyther to fable nor to lye
But I come hyther your soules to edyfye
For we freres are bounde the people to teche
The gospell of Chryst openly to preche
As dyd the appostels by Chryst theyr mayster sent
To turne the people and make them to repent
But syth the appostels fro heueu[1] wolde not come
We freres now must occupy theyr rome
We freres are bounde to serche mennes conscyens
We may not care for grotes nor for pens
We freres have professed wylfull pouerte
No peny in our purse haue may we

---

[1] = Heuen.

Knyfe nor staffe may we none cary
Excepte we shulde from the gospell vary
For worldly aduersyte may we be in no sorowe
We may not care to day for our meate to morowe
Bare fote and bare legged must we go also
We may not care for frost nor snowe
We may have no maner care ne thynke
Nother for our meate nor for our drynke
But let our thoughtes fro suche thynges be as free
As be the byrdes that in the ayre flee
For why our lorde clyped swete Jesus
In the gospell speketh to us thus
Through all the worlde go ye sayth he
And to euery creature speke ye of me
And shew of my doctryne and connynge
And that they may be glad of your comynge
Yf that you enter in any hous any where
Loke that ye salute them and byd my peas be there
And yf that house be worthy and electe
Thylke peace there than shall take effecte
And yf that hous be cursyd or paruert
Thylke peace than shall to your selfe reuert
And furthermore yf any suche there be
Which do deny for to receyue ye
And do dyspyse your doctryne and your lore
At suche a house tary ye no more
And from your shoes scrape away the dust
To theyr reprefe and I both trew and iust
Shall vengeaunce take of theyr synfull dede
    Wherfore my frendes to this text take ye hede
Beware how ye despyse the pore freres
Which ar in this worlde crystes mynysters
But do them with an harty chere receyue
Leste they happen your houses for to leue
And then god wyll take vengeaunce in his yre

Wherfore I now that am a pore frere
Dyd enquere were any people were
Which were dysposyd the worde of god to here
And as I cam hether one dyd me tell
That in this towne ryght good folke dyd dwell
Which to here the worde of god wolde be glad
And as sone as I therof knowlege had
I hyder hyed me as fast as I myght
Entendyd by the grace of god almyght
And by your pacyens and supportacyon
Here to make a symple colacyon
Wherfore I requyre all ye in this prese
For to abyde and gyue dew audyence
    But fyrst of all
Now here I shall
To god my prayer make
    To gyue ye grace
All in thys place
His doctryne for to take
          And than kneleth downe the frere sayenge his
          prayers and in the mean whyle entreth the par-
          doner with all his relyques to declare what eche
          of them ben and the hole power and vertu therof.

THE PARDONER

    God and saynt Leonarde sende ye all his grace
As many as ben assembled in this place
    Good deuoute people that here do assemble
I pray good that ye may all well resemble
The ymage after whiche you are wrought
And that ye saue that Chryst in you bought
    Deuoute Chrysten people ye shall all wytte
That I am comen hyther ye to vysytte
Wherfore let us pray thus or I begynne
Our sauyoure preserve ye all from synne

And enable ye to receyue this blessed pardon
Whiche is the greatest under the son
Graunted by the pope in his bulles under lede
Whiche pardon ye shall fynde whan ye are dede
That offereth outher grotes or els pens
To these holy relyques which or I go hens
I shall here shewe in open audyence
Exortynge ye all to do to them reuerence
    But fyrst ye shall knowe well yt I com fro Rome
Lo here my bulles all and some
Our lyege lorde seale here on my patent
There with me my body to warant
That no man be so bolde be he preest or clarke
Me to dysturbe of Chrystes holy warke
Nor have no dysdayne nor yet scorne
Of these holy relyques whiche sayntes haue worne
    Fyrst here I shewe ye of a holy Jewes shepe
A bone I pray you take good kepe
To my wordes and marke them well
Yf any of your bestes belyes do swell
Dyppe this bone in the water that he dothe take
Into his body and the swellynge shall slake
And yf any worme haue your beestes stonge
Take of this water and wasshe his tonge
And it wyll be hole anon and furthermore
Of pockes and scabbes and every sore
He shall be quyte hole that drynketh of the well
That this bone is dipped in it is treuth that I tell
And yf any man that any beste oweth
Ones in the weke or that the cocke croweth
Fastynge wyll drynke of this well a draughte
As that holy Jew hath us taught
His beestes and his store shall multeply
And maysters all its helpeth well
Thoughe a man be foule in ielous rage
Let a man with this water make his potage

And neuermore shall he his wyfe mystryst
Thoughe he in sothe the faut by her wyst
Or hab[1] she be take with freres two or thre
    Here is a mytten eke as ye may se
He that his hande wyll put in this myttayn
He shall haue encrease of his grayn
That he hathe sowne be it wete or otys
So that he offer pens or els grotes
And another holy relyke eke here se ye may
The blessed arme of swete saynt sondaye
And who so euer is blessyd with this ryght hande
Can not spede amysse by se nor by lande
And yf he offereth eke with good devocyon
He shall not fayle to come to hyghe promocyon
    And another holy relyke here may ye see
The great too of the holy trynyte
And who so euer ones dothe it in his mouthe take
He shall neuer be dysseasyd with the tothe ake
Canker nor pockys shall there none brede
This that I shewe ye is matter in dede
    And here is of our lady a relyke full good
Her bongrace which she ware with her french
    hode
Whan she wente oute alwayes for sonne bornyng
Women with chylde which be in mournynge
By vertue therof shalbe sone easyd
And of theyr trauayll full sone also releasyd
And yf this bongrace they do deuoutly kys
And offer therto as theyr deuocyon is
    Here is another relyke eke a precyous one
Of all helowes the blessyd jaw bone
Which relyke without any fayle
Agaynst poyson chefely dothe preuayle
For whom so euer it toucheth without dout
All maner venym from hym shall issue out

[1] = had.

So that it shall hurt no maner wyghte
Lo of this relyke the great power and myghte
Which preseruyth from poyson every man
Lo of saynt Myghell eke the brayn pan
Which for the hed ake is a preseruatyfe
To euery man or beste that beryth lyfe
And further it shall stande hym in better stede
For his hede shall neuer ake whan that he is dede
Nor he shall fele no maner grefe nor payn
Though with a sworde one cleve it than a twayn
But be as one that lay in a dede slepe
Wherfore to these relykes now com crouche and crepe
But loke that ye offerynge to them make
Or els can ye no maner profyte take
But one thynge ye women all I warant you
Yf any wyght be in this place now
That hathe done syn so horryble that she
Dare nat for shame therof shryuen be
Or any woman be she yonge or olde
That hathe made her husbande cockolde
Suche folke shall haue no power nor no grace
To offer to my relykes in this place
And who so fyndyth her selfe out of suche blame
Com hyther to me on crystes holy name
    And bycause ye
Shall unto me
Gyve credence at the full
Myn auctoryte
Now shall ye se
Lo here the popes bull

        Now shall the frere begyn his sermon and euyn
        at the same tyme the pardoner begynneth also
        to shew and speke of his bullys and auctorytes
        com from Rome

THE FRERE

Date et dabitur vobis
Good deuout people this place of scrypture

PARDO.

Worshypfull maysters ye shall understand

FRERE

Is to you that haue no litterature

PARDO.

That pope Leo the x. hath graunted with his hand

FRERE.

Is to say in our englysshe tonge

PAR.

And by his bulles confyrmed under lede

FRERE.

As departe your goodes the poor folke amonge

PARDO.

To all maner people bothe quycke and dede

FRERE.

And god shall than gyue unto you agayne

PARDO.

Ten thousande yeres et as many lentes of pardon

FRERE.

This in the gospell so is wryten playne

PARDO.

Whan they are dede theyr soules for to guardon

FRERE.

Therefore gyue your almes in the largest wyse

PARDO.

That wyll with theyr peny or almes dede

FRERE.

Kepe not your goodes fye fye on couetyse

PARDO.

Put to theyr handes to the good spede

FRERE.

That synne with god is most abhomynable

PARDO.

Of the holy chapell of swete saynt Leonarde

FRERE.

And is eke the synne that is most damynable

PARDO.

Whiche late by frye was destroyed and marde

FRERE

In scrypture eke but I say syrs how

PARDO.

Ay by the mas one can not here

FRERE.

What a bablynge maketh yonder felow

PARDO.

For the bablynge of yonder folysshe frere

FRERE.

In scrypture eke is there many a place

PARDO.

And also maysters as I was aboute to tell

FRERE.

Which sheweth that many a mā so far forth lacketh grace

PARDO.

Pope July yᵉ vi. hath graūted fayre et well

FRERE.

That whan to them god hathe abundance sent

PARDO.

And doth xii thousande yeres of pardon to thē sende

FRERE.

They wolde dystrybute none to the indygent

PARDO.

That ought to this holy chapell sende

FRERE.

Wherat god hauynge great indignacyon

PARDO.

Pope Bonyface the ix also

FRERE.

Punysshed these men after a dyuers facyon

PARDO.

Pope July pope Innocent with dyuers popes mo

FRERE.

As the gospell full nobly dothe declare

PARDO.

Hathe graunted to the susteynynge of the same

FRERE.

How diues Epulus reygnynge in welfare

PARDO.

v thousand yeres of pardō to euery of you by name

FRERE.

And on his borde dysshes delycate

PARDO.

And clene remyssyon also of theyr syn

FRERE.

Pore Lazarus cam beggynge at his gate

PARDO.

As often tymes as you put in

FRERE.

Desyrynge som fode his honger to releve

PARDO.

Any monye into the pardoners cofer

FRERE.

But the rycheman nothynge wolde hym gyue

PARDO.

Or any money up unto it offer

FRERE.

Not so moche as a fewe crommys of breade

PARDO.

Or he that offeryth peny or grote

FRERE.

Wherfore pore lazarus of famyn strayth was dede

PARDO.

Or he that gyueth the pardoner a new cote

FRERE.

And angels hys soule to heuen dyd cary

PARD.

Or take of me outher ymage or letter

FRERE.

But now the tyche man of the contrary

PARDO.

Wherby thys pore chapell may fayre the better

FRERE.

Whan he was dede went to mysery and payne

PARDO.

And god wote it ys a full gracyous dede

FRERE.

Where for euermore he shall remayne

PARDO.

For whych god shall quyte you well your mede

FRERE.

In brennyng fyre whych shall neuer cease

PARDO.

Now helpe our pore chapell yf it be your wyll

FRERE.

But I say thou pardoner I byd the holde they peace

PARDO.

And I say thou frere holde thy tonge styll

FRERE.

What standest thou there all the day smatterynge

PARDO.

Mary what standyst thou there all day clatterrynge

FRERE.

Mary felow I com hyder to prech the word of god
Whych of no man may be forbode
But harde wyth scylence and good entent
For why it techeth them euydent
The very way and path that shall them lede
Even to heuen gatys as strayght as any threde
And he that lettyth the worde of god of audyence
Standeth accurst in the greate sentence
And so arte thou for enterruptyng me

[PARDO.]

Nay thou art a curst knaue and that shalt thou se
And all suche that to me make interrupcyon
The pope sendes them excommunycacyon

By hys bullys here redy to be redde
By bysshoppes and hys cardynalles confyrmed
And eke yf thou dysturbe me any thynge
Thou arte also a traytour to the kynge
For here hath he graunted me under hys brode seale
That no man yf he loue hys hele
Sholde me dysturbe or let in any wyse
And yf thou dost the kynges commaundement dispise
I shall make the be set fast by the fete
And where thou saydyst that thou arte more mete
Amonge the people here for to preche
Bycause thou dost them the very way teche
How to com to heuen above
Therin thou lyest and that shall I prove
And by good reason I shall make the bow
And knowe that I am meter than arte thou
    For thou whan thou hast taught them ones the way
Thou carest not whether they com there or nay
But what that thou hast done all togyder
And taught them the way for to com thyther
Yet all that thou canst ymagyn
Is but to use vertue and to abstayne fro syn
And yf they fall ones than thou canst no more
Thou canst not gyue them a salue for theyr sore
But these my letters be clene purgacyon
All thoughe neuer so many synnes they haue don
But whan thou hast taught them the way and all
Yet or they com there they may haue many a fall
In the way or that they com thyther
For why the way to heuen is very slydder
But I wyll teche them after another rate
For I shall brynge them to heuen gate
And be theyr gydes and conducts all thynges
And lede them thyther by the purse strynges
So that they shall not fall though that they wolde

FRERE.

Holde thy peace knaue thon[1] arte very bolde
Thou pratest in fayth even lyke a pardoner

PARDO.

Why despysest thou the popes mynyster
Maysters here I curse hym openly
And therwith warne all this hole company
By the popes great auctoryte
That ye leue hym and herken unto me
For tyll he be assoyled his wordes take none effecte
For out of holy chyrche he is now clene reiecte

FRERE.

My maysters he dothe but gest and raue
It forseth not for the wordes of a knave
But to the worde of god do reuerence
And here me forthe with dewe audyence

FRERE.

Maysters I shewed you ere whyle of almes dede

PARDO.

Maysters this pardon whiche I shewed you before

FRERE.

And how ye shulde gyue poore folke at theyr nede

PARDO.

Is the greatest that euer was syth god was bore

FRERE.

And yf of your partes that thynge ones were don

[1] = thou.

FRERE.

For why without confessyon or contrycyon

PARDO.

Dout not but god sholde gyue you retrybucyon

FRERE.

By this shall ye have clene remyssyon

PARDO.

But now further it ought to be declared

FRERE.

And forgyuen of the synnes seuen
Who be thes pore folke that shold haue your reward

PARDO.

Come to this pardon yf ye wyll come to heuen

FRERE.

Who be those pore folk of whome I speke et name

PARDO.

Come to this pardon yf ye wyll be in blys

FRERE.

Certes we pore freres are the same

PARDO.

This is the pardon which ye can not mysse

FRERE.

We freres dayly take payn I say

PARDO.

This is the pardon which shall mens soules wyn

L

FRERE.

We frears dayly do bothe fast and pray

PARDO.

This is the pardon the rydder of your synne

FRERE.

We freres trauayle and labour euery houre

PARDO.

This is the pardon that purchaseth all grace

FRERE.

We freres take payne for the loue of our sauyour

PARDO.

This is a pardon for all maner of trespas

FRERE.

We freres also go on lymytacyon

PARDO.

This is ye pardō of which all mercy dothe sprynge

FRERE.

For to preche to every crysten nacyon

PARDO.

This is the pardon that to heuen shall ye brynge

FRERE.

But I say thou pardoner thou wylt kepe sylens sone

PARDO.

Ye it is lyke to be whan I haue done

FRERE.

Mary therefore the more knaue thou art I say
That parturbest the worde of god I say
For neyther they selfe wylt here goddys doctryne
Ne suffre other theyr earys to enclyne
Wherfore our sauyour in his holy scrypture
Gyueth the thy iugement thou cursyd creature
Spekynge to the after this maner
Maledictus qui audit verbum dei negligenter
Wo be that man sayth our lord that gyueth no audiens
Or heryth the worde of god with negligens

PARDO.

Now thou haste spoken all syr daw
I care nat for the an olde straw
I had leuer thou were hanged up with a rope
Than I that am comen from the pope
And thereby goddes minister whyle thou stādest et prate
Sholde be fayn to knocke without the gate
Therfore preche hardely thy belyfull
But I neuerthe les wyll declare the popes bull

FRERE.

Now my frendes I haue afore shewed ye

PARDO.

Now my maysters as I haue afore declared

FRERE.

That good it is to gyue your charyte

PARDO.

That pardoners from you may not be spared

FRERE.

And further I haue at lengthe to you tolde

PARDO.

Now here after shall folow and ensew

FRERE.

Who be these people that ye receyue sholde

PARDO.

That foloweth of pardons the great vertew

FRERE.

That is to say us freres pore

PARDO.

We pardoners for your soules be as necessary

FRERE.

That for our lyuynge must begge fro dore to dore

PARDO.

As is the meate for our bodys hungry

FRERE.

For of our own propre we haue no propre thynge

PARDO.

For pardons is the thynge that bryngeth men to heuen

FRERE.

But that we get of deuout peoples gettynge

PARDO.

Pardons delyuereth them fro the synnes seuen

FRERE.

And in our place be fryers thre score and thre

PARDO.

Pardons for euery cryme may dyspens

FRERE.

Which onely lyue on mens charyte

PARDO.

Pardon purchasyth grace for all offence

FRERE.

For we fryars wylfull charyte professe

PARDO.

Ye though ye had slayne bothe father and mother

FRERE.

We may haue no money nother more nor lesse

PARDO.

And this pardon is chefe aboue all other

FRERE.

For wordly treasure we may nought care

PARDO.

For who to it offeryth grote or peny

FRERE.

Our soules must be ryche and our bodyes bare

PARDO.

Though synnes he had done never so many

FRERE.

And one thynge I had almoste left behynde

PARDO.
And though that he had all his kyndred slayn

FRERE.
Which before cam not to my mynde

PARDO.
This pardon shall ryd the frō euer lastynge payne

FRERE.
And doutles it is none other thynge

PARDO.
There is no syn so abhomynable

FRERE.
But whan ye wyll gyue your almes et offerynge

PARDO.
Which to remyt this pardon is not able

FRERE.
Loke that ye dystrybute it wysely

PARDO.
As well declareth the sentence of this letter

FRERE.
Not to euery man that for it wyll crye

PARDO.
Ye can not therefore bestow your money better

FRERE.
For yf ye gyue your almes in that wyse

PARDO.

Let us not here stande ydle all the daye

FRERE.

It shall not bothe to them and us suffyse

PARDO.

Gyue us some money or that we go our way

FRERE.

But I say thou lewde felowe thou
Haddest none other tyme to shewe thy bulles but nowe
Canst not tary and abyde tyll sone
And rede them than whan prechynge is done

PARDO.

I wyll rede them now what sayest thou therto
Hast thou any thynge therwith to do
Thynkest that I wyll stande et tary for thy leasure
Am I bounde to do so moche for thy pleasure

FRERE.

For my pleasure nay I wolde thou knewyst it well
It becometh the knaue neuer a dell
To prate thus boldely in my presence
And let the worde of god of audience

PARDO.

Let the word of god qd a nay let a horsō dreuyll[1]
Prate here all day with a foule euyll
And all thy sermon goth on couetyce
And byddest men beware of auaryce
And yet in thy sermon dost thou none other thynge
But for almes stande all the day beggynge

[1] = devil.

FRERE.

Leue thy realynge I wolde the aduyse

PARDO.

Nay leue thou thy bablynge yf thou be wyse

FRERE.

I wolde thou knewest it knaue I wyll not leue a whyt

PARDO.

No more wyll I I do the well to wyt

FRERE.

It is not thou shall make me holde my peas

PARDO.

Thā speke on hardly yf thou thynkyst it for thy eas

FRERE.

For I wyll speke whyther thou wylt or no

PARDO.

In faythe I care not for I wyll speke also

FRERE.

Wherfore hardely let us bothe go to

PARDO.

Se whiche shall be better harde of us two

FRERE.

What sholde ye gyue ought to pratyng pardoners

PARDO.

What sholde ye spende on these flaterynge lyers

FRERE.

What sholde ye gyue ought to these bolde beggars

PARDO.

As be these bablynge monkes and these freres

FRERE.

Let them hardely labour for theyr lyuynge

PARDO.

Which do nought dayly but bable and lye

FRERE.

It moche hurtyth them good mennys gyuynge

PARDO.

And tell you fables dere inoughe a flye

FRERE.

For that maketh them ydle and slouthfull to warke

PARDO.

As dothe this bablynge frere here to day

FRERE.

That for none other thynge they wyll carke

PARDO.

Dryue hym hence therfore in the xx deuyll waye

FRERE.

Hardely they wolde go bothe to plow et carte

PARDO.

On us pardoners hardely do your cost

FRERE.

And if of necessitie ones they felte the smarte

PARDO.

For why your money neuer can be lost

FRERE.

But we freres be nat in lyke estate

PARDO.

For why there is in our fraternitie

FRERE.

For our handes with such thinges we may not maculate

PARDO.

For all bretheren et sisteren that thereof be

FRERE.

We freres be nat in lyke condicion

PARDO.

Deuoutly songe euery yere

FRERE.

We may haue no prebendes ne exhibition

PARDO.

As he shall know well that cometh there

FRERE.

Of all temporal seruice are we forbode

PARDO.

At euery of the fyue solempne festes

FRERE.

And onely bounde to the seruice of god

PARDO.

A masse et dirige to pray for the good rest

FRERE.

And tnerwith to pray for euery christen nation

PARDO.

Of the soules of the bretheren et sisteren all

FRERE.

That god witsafe to saue them fro dampnation

PARDO.

Of our fraternitie in generall

FRERE.

But some of you so harde be of harte

PARDO.

With a herse there standynge well arayed et dyght

FRERE.

Ye can not wepe though ye full sore smarte

PARDO.

And torches et tapers aboute it brennynge bright

FRERE.

Wherfore some man must ye hyre nedes

PARDO.

And with the belles eke solemnpnely ryngynge

FRERE.

Whiche must intrete god for your misdedes

PARDO.

And prestes et clerkes deuoutly syngynge

FRERE.

Ye can hyre no better in myne oppinion

PARDO.

And furthermore euery nyght in the yere

FRERE.

Than us goddes seruantes men of religion

PARDO.

Twelve pore people are receiued there

FRERE.

And specially god hereth us pore freres

PARDO.

And there haue bothe harborow and food

FRERE.

And is attentife unto our desyres

PARDO.

That for them is conuenient and good

FRERE.

For the more of religion the more herde of our lorde

PARDO.

And furthermore if there be any other

❡ A mery playe betwene

the pardoner and the frere the curate
and neybour Pratte.

❡ The frere.

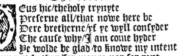

Eus hic/the holy trynyte
preserue all/that nowe here be
Dere bretherne/yf ye wyll consyder
The cause why/I am come hyder
Ye wolde be glad/to knowe my intent
for I com not hyther/for monye nor for rent
I com not hyther/for meate nor for meale
But I com hyther/for your soules heale
I com not hyther/to poll nor to shaue
I com not hyther to begge nor to craue
I com not hyther/to glose nor to flatter
I com not hyther to bable nor to clatter
I com not hyther/to fable nor to lye
But I com hyther/youe soules to edyfye
for we freres/are bounde the people to teche
The gospell of Chryst/openly to preche
As dyd the apposteles by Chryst theyr mayster sent
To turne the people/and make them to repent
But syth the apposteles/fro heuen wolde not come
We freres nowe/must occupy theyr rome
We freres are bounde/to serche mennes conscyens
We may not care for grotes/nor for pens
We freres haue professed/wylfull pouerte
No peny in our purse/haue may we
Knyfe nor staffe/may we none cary
Excepte we shulde/from the gospell vary
for worldly aduersyte/may we be in no sorowe
We may not care to day/for our meate to morowe
Bare fote and bare legged/must we go also
We may not care/for frost nor snowe
We may haue/no maner care ne thynke
Nother for our meate/nor for our drynke
But let our thoughtes/fro suche thynges be as free
As be the byrdes/that in the ayre flee
for why our lorde/clyped swete Jesus
In the gospell/speketh to vs thus

A.i.

(See pages 147 and 148)

FRERE.

And that is so shulde good reason doeth accorde

PARDO.

That of our fraternitie be sister or brother

FRERE.

Therfore doute nat maisters I am euen he

PARDO.

Whiche hereafter happé to fall in decay

FRERE.

To whom ye shulde parte with your charitie

PARDO.

And yf he than chaunce to come that way

FRERE.

We freres be they that shulde your almes take

PARDO.

Nygh unto our forsayd holy place

FRERE.

Which for your soules helth do both watche et wake

PARDO.

Ye shall there tary for a monethes space

FRERE.

We freres pray god wote whan ye do slepe

PARDO.

And be there founde of the places cost

FRERE.

We for your synnes do bothe sobbe and wepe

PARDO.

Wherfore now in the name of the holy goost

FRERE.

To pray to god for mercy and for grace

PARDO.

I aduise you all that now here be

FRERE.

And thus do we dayly with all our hole place

PARDO.

For to be of our fraternitie

FRERE.

Wherfore distribute of your temporall welthe

PARDO.

Fye on couetise sticke nat for a peny

FRERE.

By whiche ye may preserue your soules helthe

PARDO.

For whiche ye may haue benefites so many

FRERE.

I say wylt thou not yet stynt thy clappe
Pull me downe the pardoner with an euyll happe

PARDO.

Maister frere I holde it best
To kepe your tonge while ye be in rest

FRERE.

I say one pull the knaue of his stole

PARDO.

Nay one pull the frere downe lyke a fole

FRERE.

Leue thy railynge and babbelynge of freres
Or by Jys I sh[all] lug the by the swete eares

PARDO.

By god I wolde thou durst presume to it

FRERE.

By god a lytell thynge might make me to do it

PARDO.

And I shrew thy herte and thou spare

FRERE.

By god I wyll nat mysse the moche thou slouche
And if thou playe me suche another touche
Ish knocke the on the costarde I wolde thou it knewe

PARDO.

Mary that wolde I se quod blynde hew

FRERE.

Well I wyll begyn and than let me se
Whether thou darest agayne interrupte me
And what thou wolde ones to it say

PARDO.

Begyn et proue whether I wyll ye or nay

FRERE.

And to go forthe where as I lefte right now

PARDO.

Because som percase wyll thynke amysse of me

FRERE.

Our lorde in the gospell sheweth the way how

PARDO.

Ye shall now here the popys auctoryte

FRERE.

By gogges soule knaue I suffre the no lenger

PARDO.

I say some good body lende me his hengar
And I shall hym teche by god almyght
How he shall another tyme lerne for to fyght
I shall make that balde crown of his to loke rede
I shall leue hym but one ere on his hede

FRERE.

But I shall eue the neuer an ere or I go

PARDO.

Ye horeson frere wylt thou so
                                Than the fyght

FRERE.

Lose thy handes away from myn earys

M

PARDO.

Than take thou thy handes away from my heres
Nay abyde thou horeson I am not downe yet
I trust fyrst to lye the at my fete

FRERE.

Ye horeson wylt thou scrat and byte

PARDO.

Ye mary wyll I as longe as thou doste smyte

THE CURATE

PARSŌ.

Holde your handes a vengeaunce on ye bothe two
that euer ye came hyther to make this a do
To polute my chyrche a myschyefe on you lyght
I swere to you by god all myght
Ye shall bothe repente euery vayne of your harte
As sore as ye dyd euer thynge or ye departe

FRERE.

Mayster parson I maruayll ye wyll gyue lycence
To this false knaue in this audience
To publysh his ragman rolles with lyes
I desyred hym y wys more than ones or twyse
To holde his peas tyll that I had done
But he wolde here no more than the man in the mone

PARDO.

Why sholde I suffre the more than thou me
Mayster parson gaue me lycence before the
And I wolde thou knewyst it I haue relykes here
Other maner stuffe than thou dost bere

I wyll edefy more with the syght of it
Than wyll all the pratynge of holy wryt
For that except that the precher hym selfe lyue well
His predycacyon wyll helpe neuer a dell
And I know well that thy lyuynge is nought
Thou art an apostata yf it were well sought
An homycyde thou art I know well inoughe
For my selfe knew where thou sloughe
A wench with thy dagger in a couche
And yet as thou saist in thy sermō yt no mā shall touch

PARSŌ.

No more of this wranglyng in my chyrch
I shrewe your hertys bothe for this lurche
Is there any blood shed here betwen these knaues
Thanked be god they had no stauys
Nor egoteles for than it had ben wronge
Well ye shall syuge[1] another songe
Neybour prat com hether I you pray

PRAT.

Why what is this nyse fraye

PARSŌ.

I can not tell you one knaue dysdaynes another
Wherfore take ye the tone and I shall take the other
We shall bestow them there as is most conuenyent
For suche a couple I trow they shall repente
That euer they met in this chyrche here
Neyboure ye be constable stande ye nere
Take ye that laye knaue and let me alone
With this gentylman by god and by saynt John
I shall borowe upon prestholde somwhat
For I may say to the neybour prat

[1] . = synge.

It is a good dede to punysh such to the ensample
Of suche other how that they shall mell
In lyke facyon as these catyfes do

PRAT.

In good fayth mayster parson yf ye do so
Ye do but well to teche them to beware

PARDO.

Mayster prat I pray ye me to spare
For I am sory for that that is done
Wherfore I pray ye forgyue me sone
For that I have offendyd within your lybertye
And by my trouthe syr ye may trust me
I wyll neuer come hether more
Whyle I lyue and god before

PRAT.

Nay I am ones charged with the
Wherfore by saynt John thou shalt not escape me
Tyll thou hast scouryd a pare of stokys

PARSŌ.

Tut he wenoth all is but mockes
Lay hande on hym and com ye on syr frere
Ye shall of me hardely haue your hyre
Ye had none suche this vii yere
I swere by god and by our lady dere

PARDO.

Nay mayster parson for goddys passyon
Intreate not me after that facyon
For yf ye do it wyll not be for your honesty

PARSŌ.

Honesty or not but thou shall se
What I shall do by and by
Make no stroglynge com forthe soberly
For it shall not auayle the I say

FRERE.

Mary that shall we trye euen strayt way
I defy the churle preeste et there be no mo than thou
I wyll not go with the I make god a vow
We shall se fyrst which is the stronger
God hath sent me bonys I do the not fere

PARSŌ.

Ye by thy fayth wylt thou be there
Neybour prat brynge forthe that knaue
And thou syr frere yf thou wylt algatys raue

FRERE.

Nay chorle I the defy
I shall trouble the fyrst
Thou shalt go to pryson by and by
Let me se now do thy worste

Prat with the pardoner et the parson with the frere

PARSŌ.

Helpe helpe neybour prat neybour prat
In the worshyp of god helpe me somwhat

PRAT.

Nay deale as thou canst with that elfe
For why I haue inoughe to do my selfe
Alas for payn I am almoste dede
The reede blood so ronneth downe about my hede
Nay and thou canst I pray thee help me

PARSŌ.

Nay by the mas felowe it wyll not be
I have more tow on my dystaffe thā I can well spyn
The cursed frere dothe the upper hande wyn

FRERE.

Wyll ye leue than and let us in peace departe

PS. ET PR.

Ye by our lady euen with all our harte

FRE. PD.

Than adew to the deuyll tyll we come agayn

PSŌ. PR.

And a myschefe go with you bothe twayne

Imprynted by Wyllyam Rastell the v day
of Apryll the yere of our lorde
M.CCCCC.XXXIII
Cum priuilegio

THE FOURE P.P.

NOTE ON THE EDITIONS

THE editions can be described as:

(1) *M* by *M*yddylton. This by internal evidence at the end of the play may be dated *perhaps* before 1552—i.e. the date of the Second Prayer Book—which disallowed prayers for the dead, and *certainly* before 1559.

(2) *C* by *C*opland. This by the variation of the same line belongs to 1552, or more probably 1559; as the 1552 Prayer Book was very little in use.

(3) *A* by *A*llde is dated, and its colophon 1569 concludes very significantly Q[UO]D JOHN HEYWOOD as if printed directly from a manuscript.

*   *   *   *   *

The text which I have used is that of *M* by WYLLYAM MYDDYLTON of London, which is in the British Museum and is ascribed to 1545.

I have collated it with *A* by JOHN ALLDE, also in the British Museum; and with *C* by WYLLYAM COPLAND, undated in the Bodleian. Though originally I collated the three editions meticulously I decided to reproduce *M* and neglect its multifarious divergencies from *C* and *A*, many of which are slight or obvious.

The edition which I have chosen sets out to be "newe": whereas *A* omits the word "newe," and clearly is more modern generally than *M*;.and often than *C*. I should say that *C* was taken from *M*, and *A* from *C*; or that *A* and *C* were both taken from an earlier edition than *M*.

THE PLAYE CALLED THE FOURE P.P.

A newe and a very mery enterlude of

A Palmer
A Pardoner
A Potycary
A Pedler

Made by Johñ Heewood

PALMER

Nowe God be here who kepeth this place
Now by my fayth I crye you mercy
Of reason I must sew for grace
My rewdness sheweth me no so homely
Wherof your pardon axt and wonne
I sew you as curtesy doth me bynde
To tell thys whiche shalbe begonne
In order as may come beste in myndy[1]
I am a palmer as ye se
Whiche of my lyfe much part hath spent
In many a fayre and farre countre
As pylgrymes do of good intent
At Hierusalem haue I bene
Before Chrystes blessed sepulture
The Mount of Caluery haue I sene
A holy place, ye may be sure
To Iosophat and Olyuete
On fote God wote I wente ryght bare
Many a salt tere dyde I swete
Before thys carkes coulde come there
Yet haye I bene at Rome also
And gone the stacions all arow

---

[1] = mynde.

Saynt peters shryne and many mo
    Then yf I tolde all ye do know
Except that there be any suche
    That hath ben there and diligently
Hath taken hede and marked muche
    Then can they speke as muche as I
Then at the Rodes also I was
And rounde about to Amyas
At saynt Toncomber and saynt Tronion
At saynt Bothulph and saynt Anne of Buckston;
On the hylles of Armony where I see Noes arke
With holy Iob and saynt George in Suthwarke
At Waltam and at Walsyngam
And at the good rood of dagnam
At saynt Cornelys at saynt Iames in Gales
And at saynt Wynefrydes well in Walles
At our lady of Boston at saynt Edmundes-byry
And streyght to saynt Patrykes purgatory
At rydybone and at the blood of Hayles
Where pylgrymes paynes ryght muche auayles
At saynt Dauys and at saynt Denis
At saynt Mathew and saynt Marke in Venis
At mayster Iohan shorne at Canterbury
The graet god of Katewade at kynge Henry
At saynt sauyours at our lady of Southwell
At Crome at Wylsdome and at Muswell
At saynt Rycharde and at saynt Roke
And at our lady that standeth in the oke
To these with other many one
Deuoutly haue I prayed and gone
Prayeng to them to pray for me
Unto the blessed trynyte
By whose prayers and my dayly payne
I truste the soner to obtay[n]e
For my saluacyon grace and mercy

For be ye sure I thynke surely
Who seketh sayntes for Crystes sake
And namely suche as payne do take
On fote to punyshe thy frayle body
Shall therby meryte more hyely
Then by any-thynge done by man

PARDONER

And when ye haue gone as farre as ye can
For all your labour and gostely entente
Yet welcome home as wyse as ye wente

PALMER

Why sir dyspyse ye pylgrymage

PARDONER

Nay for God syr then dyd I rage
I thynke ye ryght well occupyed
To seke these sayntes on euery syde
Also your payne I nat disprayse it
But yet I discomende your wit
And or we go euen so shall ye
If ye in this wyl answere me
I pray you shew what the cause is
Ye wente al these pylgrymages

PALMER

Forsoth this lyfe I dyd begyn
To rydde the bondage of my syn
For whiche these sayntes rehersed or this
I haue both sought and sene i-wys
Besechynge them to be recorde
Of all my payne vnto the Lorde
That gyueth all remyssyon
Upon eche mans contricyon

And by theyr good mediacyon
Upon myne humble submyssion
I trust to haue in very dede
For my soule helth the better spede

PARDONAR

Nowe is your owne confessyon lyckely
To make your-selfe a fole quyckely
For I perceyue ye wolde obtayne
No nother thynge for all your payne
But onely grace your soule to saue
Nowe marke in this what wyt ye haue
To seke so farre and helpe so nye
Euen here at home is remedy
For at your dore my-selfe doth dwell
Who coulde haue saued your soule as well
As all your wyde wandrynge shall do
Though ye wente thryes to Iericho
Nowe syns ye myght haue spedde at home
What haue ye wone by ronnyng at Rome

PALMER

If this be true that ye haue moued
Then is my wyt in-dede reproued
But let vs here fyrste what ye are

PARDONAR

Truly I am a pardoner

PALMER

Truely a pardoner that may be true
But a true pardoner doth nat ensew
Ryght selde is it sene or neuer
That treuth and pardoners dwell together
For be your pardons neuer so great
Yet them to enlarge ye wyll nat let

With suche lyes that oftymes Cryste wot
Ye seme to haue that ye haue nat
Wherfore I went my-selfe to the selfe thynge
In euery place and without faynynge
Had as muche pardon there assuredly
As ye can promyse me here doutefully
Howe-be-it I thynke ye do but scofte
But yf ye hadde all the pardon ye kepe of
And no whyt of pardon graunted
In any place where I haue haunted
Yet of my labour I nothynge repent
God hathe respect how eche tyme is spent
And as in his knowledge all is regarded
So by his goodnes all is rewarded

PARDONAR

By the fyrste parte of this laste tale
It semeth you come late from the ale
For reason on your syde so farre doth fayle
That ye leue [re]soning and begyn to rayle
Wherin ye forget your owne parte clerely
For ye be as vntrue as I
And in one poynte ye are beyonde me
For ye may lye by aucthoryte
And all that hath wandred so farre
That no man can be theyr controller
And where ye esteme your labour so muche
I say yet agayne my pardons be suche
That yf there were a thousande soules on a hepe
I wolde brynge them all to heyen as good chepe
As ye haue brought your-selfe on pylgrymage
In the leste quarter of your vyage
Which is farre a thys side heuen by god
There your labour and pardon is od

With smale cost and without any payne
These pardons bryngeth them to heuen playne
Geue me but a peny or two pens
And as sone as the soule departeth hens
In halfe an hour or thre quarters at moste
The soule is in heuen with the Holy Ghost

POTYCARY

Sende ye any soules to heuen by water

PARDONER

If we dyd syr what is the mater

POTYCARY

By God I haue a drye soule shulde thyther
I praye you let our soules go to heuen togyther
So bysy you twayne be in soules helth
May nat a potycary come in by stelth
Yes that I wyll by saynt Antony
And by the leue of thys company
Proue ye false knaues both or we goo
In parte of your sayenges as thys lo
Thou by thy trauayle thynkest heyen to gete
And thou by pardons and relyques countest no lete
To sende thyne owne soule to heyen sure
And all other whome thou lyste to procure
If I toke an accyon then were they blanke
For lyke theues the knaues rob away my thanke
All soules in heuen hauynge relefe
Shall they thanke your craftes nay thanke myn chefe
No soule ye knowe entreth heuen gate
Tyll from the bodye he be separate
And whom haue ye knowen dye ho[ne]stlye
Without helpe of the potycary

Nay all that commeth to our handlynge
Except ye happe to come to hangynge
That way perchaunce ye shall nat myster
To go to heuen without a glyster
But be ye sure I wolde be wo
If ye shulde chaunge to begyle me so
As good to lye with me a-nyght
As hange abrode in the mone lyght
There is no choyse to fle my hande
But as I sayd into the bande
Syns of our soules the multitude
I sende to heuen when all is vewed
Who shulde but I then all-togyther
Haue thanke of all theyr commynge thyther

PARDONER

If ye kylde a thousande in an houre space
When come they to heuen dyenge from state of grace

POTYCARY

If a thousande pardons about your neckes were teyd
When come they to heuen yf they neyer dyed

PALMER

Longe lyfe after good workes in-dede
Doth hynder mannes receyt of mede
And deth before one dewty done
May make vs thynke we dye to sone
Yet better tary a thynge then haue it
Then go to sone and vaynly craue it

PARDONER

The longer ye dwell in communicacion
The lesse shall you lyke thys ymagynacyon

For ye may perceyve euen at the fyrst chop
Your tale is trapt in such a stop
That at the leste ye seme worse then we

POTYCARY

By the masse I holde vs nought all thre

PEDLER

By our lady then haue I gone wronge
And yet to be here I thought longe

POTYCARY

Brother ye haue gone wronge no wyt
I prayse your fortune and your wyt
That can dyrecte you so discretely
To plante you in this company
Thou palmer and thou a pardoner
I a potycary

PEDLER

And I a pedler

POTYCARY

Nowe on my fayth full well watched
Were the deuyll were we foure hatched

PEDLER

That maketh no mater syns we be matched
I coulde be mery yf that I catchyd
Some money for parte of the ware in my packe

POTYCARY

What the deuyll hast thou there at thy backe

PEDLER

Why dost thou nat knowe that every pedled[1]
In euery tryfull must be a medler
Specyally in womens tryflynges
Those vse we chefe aboue all thynges
Whiche thynges to se yf ye be disposed
Beholde what ware here is disclosed
Thys gere sheweth it-selfe in such bewte
That eche man thynketh it sayth come bye me
Loke were your-selfe can luke to be chooser
Your-selfe shall make pryce though I be looser
Is here nothynge for my father Palmer
Haue ye nat a wanton in a corner
For your walkyng to holy places
By cryste I haue herde of as straunge cases
Who lyueth in loue or loue wolde wynne
Euen at this packe he must begynne
Where is ryght many a proper token
Oh whiche by name parte shall be spoken
Gloues pynnes combes glasses vnspottyd
Pomanders hookes and lasses knotted
Broches rynges and all maner bedes
Lace rounde and flat for womens hedes
Nedyls threde thymbell shers and all suche knackes
Where louers be no suche thynges lackes
Sypers swathbondes rybandes and sleue-laces
Gyrdyls knyues purses and pyncases

POTYCARY

Do women bye theyr pyncases of you

PEDLER

Ye that they do I make God a vow

[1] = pedler.

N

POTYCARY

So mot I thryue then for my parte
I be-shrewe thy knaues nakyd herte
For makynge my wyfys pyncase so wyde
The pynnes fall out they can nat abyde
Great pynnes must she haue one or other
Yf she lese one she wyll fynde an-other
Wherin I fynde cause to complayne
New pynnes to her pleasure and my payne

PARDONER

Syr ye came well sene in womens causes
I praye you tell me what causeth this
That women after theyr arysynge
Be so longe in theyr apparelynge

PEDLER

Forsoth women haue many lettes
And they be masked in many nettes
As frontlettes fyllettes parlettes and barcelettes
And then theyr bonettes and theyr poynettes
By these lettes and nettes the lette is suche
That spede is small whan haste is muche

POTYCARY

An-other cause why they come nat forwarde
Whiche maketh them dayly to drawe backwarde
And yet is a thynge they can nat forbere
The trymmynge and pynnynge vp theyr gere
Specyally theyr fydlyng with the tayle-pyn
And when they wolde haue it prycke in
If it chaunce to double in the clothe
Then be they wode and swereth an othe
Tyll it stande ryght they wyll nat forsake it
Thus though it may nat yet wolde they make it

But be ye sure they do but defarre it
For when they wolde make it ofte tymes marre it
But prycke them and pynne them as nyche[1] as ye wyll
And yet wyll they loke for pynnynge styll
So that I durste holde you a Toynt
Ye shall neuer haue them at a fall poynt

PEDLER

Let womens maters passe and marke myne
What-euer theyr poyntes be these poyntes be fyne
Wherfore yf ye be wyllynge to bye
Ley downe money come of quyckely

PALMER

Nay by my trouth we be lyke fryers
We are but beggers we be no byers

PARDONER

Syr ye maye showe your ware for your mynde
But I thynke ye shall no profyte fynde

PEDLER

Well though thys yourney acquyte no coste
Yet thynke I nat my labour loste
For by the fayth of my body
I lyke full well thys company
Up shall this packe for it is playne
I came not hyther al for gayne
Who may nat play one day in a weke
May thynke hys thryfte is farre to seke
Deuyse what pastyme ye thynke beste
And make ye sure to fynde me prest

POTYCARY

Why be ye so vnyuersall
That you can do what-so-euer ye shall

---

[1] = myche.

PEDLER

Syr yf ye lyst to appose me
What I can do then shall ye se

POTYCARY

Then tell me thys be ye perfyt in drynkynge

PEDLER

Perfyt in drynkynge as may be wysht by thynkyng

POTYCARY

Then after your drynkyng how fall ye to wynkyng

PEDLER

Syr after drynkynge whyle the shot is tynkynge
Some hedes be swymmyng byt myne wyl be synkynge
And vpon drynkynge myne eyse wyll be pynkynge
For wynkynge to drynkynge is alway lynkynge

POTYCARY

Then drynke and slepe ye can well do
But yf ye were desyred therto
I pray you tell me can you synge

PEDLER

Syr I haue some syght in syngynge

POTYCARY

But is your brest any-thynge swete

PEDLER

What-euer my breste be my voyce is mete

POTYCARY

That answer sheweth you a ryght syngynge man
Now what is your wyll good father than

PALMER

What helpeth wyll where is no skyll

PARDONER

And what helpeth skyll where is no wyt

POTYCARY

For wyll or skyll what helpeth it
Where frowarde knaues be lackynge wyll
Leue of thys curyosytie
And who that lyste synge after me

Here they synge˙

PEDLER

Thys lyketh me well so mot I the

PARDONER

So helpe me God it lyketh nat me
Where company is met and well agreed
Good pastyme doth ryght well in-dede
But who can syt in dalyaunce
Men syt in suche a variaunce
As we were set or ye came in
Whiche stryfe thys man dyd fyrst begynne
Allegynge that such men as use
For loue of God nat and[1] refuse
On fot to goo from place to place
A pylgrymage callynge for grace
Shall in that payne with penitence
Obtayne discharge of conscyence
Comparynge that lyfe for the beste
Enduccyon to our endles reste
Upon these wordes our mater grewe
For yf he coulde auow them true

[1] nat and = and nat.

As good to be a gardener
As for to be a pardoner
But when I harde hym so farre wyde
I then aproched and replyed
Sayenge this that this indulgence
Hauyng the forsayd penitence
Dyschargeth man of all offence
With muche more profyt then this pretence
I aske but two pens at the moste
I-wys this is nat very great coste
And from all payne without dyspayre
My soule for his kepe euen his chayre
And when he dyeth he may be sure
To come to heuen euen at pleasure
And more then heuen he can nat get
How farre so-euer he lyste to iet
Then in hys payne more then hys wit
To wa[l]ke to heuen syns he may syt
Syr as we were in this contencion
In came thys daw with hys inuencyon
Reuelynge vs hym-selfe auauntynge
That all the soules to heuen assendynge
Are most bounde to the potycary
Bycause he helpeth most men to dye
Before whiche deth he sayeth in-dede
No soule in heuen can haue hys mede

PEDLER

Why do potycaries kyll men

POTYCARY

By God men say so now and then

PEDLER

And I thought ye wolde nat haue myst
To make men lyue as longe as ye lyste

POTYCARY

As longe as we lyste nay longe as they can

PEDLER

So myght we lyue without you than

POTYCARY

Ye but yet it is necessary
For to haue a potycary
For when ye fele your conscyens redy
I can sende you to heuen quyckly
Wherfore concernynge our mater here
Aboue these twayne I am best clere
And yf ye lyste to take me so
I am content you and no mo
Shall be our iudge as in thys case
Whiche of vs thre shall take the best place

PEDLER

I neyther wyll iudge the beste nor worste
For be ye bleste or be ye curste
Ye know it is no whyt my Sleyght
To be a iudge in maters of weyght
It behoueth no pedlers nor proctours
To take on them iudgemente as doctours
But yf your myndes be onely set
To worke for soule helthe ye be well met
For eche of you somwhat doth showe
That soules towarde heuen by you do growe
Then yf ye can so well agree
To contynue togyther all thre
And all you thre obey on wyll
Then all your myndes ye may fulfyll
As yf ye came all to one man
Who shulde goo pylgrymage more then he can

In that ye palmer as debite
May clerely dyscharde¹ hym parde
And for all other syns ones had contryssyon
Your pardons geueth hym full remyssyon
And then ye mayster potycary
May sende hym to heuen by-and-by

POTYCARY

Yf he taste this boxe nye aboute the pryme
By the masse he is in heuen or euensonge tyme
My craft is suche that I can ryght well
Sende my fryndes to heuen and my-selfe to hell
But syrs marke this man for he is wyse
How coulde deuyse suche a deuyce
For yf we thre may be as one
Then be we lordes euerychone
Betwene vs all coulde nat be myste
To saue the soules of whome we lyste
But for good order at a worde
Twayne of vs must wayte on the thyrde
And vnto that I do agree
For bothe you twayne shall wayt on me
   What chaunce is this that suche an elfe
Commauned two knaues besyde hym-selfe

[PARDONER]

Nay nay my frende that wyll nat be
I am to good to wayt on the

PALMER

By our lady and I wolde be loth
To wayt on the better on you both

¹ = dyscharge.

PEDLER

Yet be ye sewer for all thys dout
Thys waytynge must be brought about
Men can nat prosper wylfully ledde
All thynge decayed where is no hedde
Wherfore doutlesse marke what I say
To one of you thre twayne must obey
And synnes ye can nat agree in voyce
Who shall be hed there is no choyse
But to deuyse some maner thynge
Wherin ye all be lyke connynge
And in the same who can do beste
The other twayne to make them preste
In euery thynge of hys entente
Holly to be at commaundement
And now haue I founde one mastry
That ye can do in-dyfferently
And is nother sellynge nor byenge
But euyn only very lyenge
And all ye thre can lye as well
As can the falsest deuyll in hell
And though afore ye harde me grudge
In greater maters to be your iudge
Yet in lyeng I can some skyll
And yf I shall be iudge I wyll
And be ye sure without flatery
Where my consciens fyndeth the mastrye
Ther shall my iudgement strayt be founde
Though I myght wynne a thousande pounde

PALMER

Syr for lyeng though I can do it
Yet am I loth for to goo to it

PEDLER

Ye haue nat cause to feare to be bolde
For ye may be here vncontrolled
And ye in this haue good auauntage
For lyeng is your comen vsage
And you in lyenge be well spedde
For all your craft doth stande in falshed
Ye nede nat care who shall begyn
For eche of you may hope to wyn
Now speke all thre euyn as ye fynde
Be ye agreed to folowe my mynde

PALMER

Ye by my trouth I am content

PARDONER

Now in good fayth and I assente

POTYCARY

If I denyed I were a nody
For all is myne by goddes body

Here the Potycary hoppeth

PALMER

Here were a hopper to hop for the rynge
But syr thys gere goth nat by hoppynge

POTYCARY

Syr in this hopynge I wyll hop so well
That my tonge shall hop as well as my hele
Upon whiche hoppynge I hope and nat doute it
To hope so that ye shall hope without [it]

PALMER

Syr I wyll neyther boste ne brawll
But take suche fortune as may fall
And yf ye wynne this maystry
I wyll obaye you quietly
And sure I thynke that quietnesse
In any man is great rychesse
In any maner company
To rule or be ruled indifferently

PARDONER

By that bost thou semest a begger in-dede
What can thy quyetnesse helpe vs at nede
Yf we shulde starue thou hast nat I thynke
One peny to bye vs one potte of drynke
Nay yf rychesse mygh[t]e rule the roste
Beholde what cause I haue to boste
Lo here be pardons halfe a dosyn
For gostely ryches they haue no cosyn
And more-ouer to me they brynge
Sufficient succour for my lyuynge
And here be relykes of suche a kynde
As in this worlde no man can fynde
Knele downe all thre and when ye leue kyssynge
Who lyste to offer shall haue my blyssynge
Frendes here shall ye se euyn anone
Of All-Hallows the blessyd iaw-bone
Kys it hardely with good deuocion

POTYCARY

This kysse shall brynge vs much promocyon
Fogh by saynt sauyour I neuer kyst a wars
Ye were as good kysse all-hallows ars
For by all-halows me thynketh
That all-halows breth stynkith

PALMER

Ye iudge all-halows breth vnknowen
Yf any brethe stynke it is your owne

POTYCARY

I knowe myne owne breth from all-halows
Or els it were tyme to kysse the galows

PARDONER

Nay syrs beholde here may ye se
The great-toe of the trinite
Who to thys toe any money voweth
And ones may role it in his moueth
All hys lyfe after I vndertake
He shall be ryd of the toth-ake

POTYCARY

I praye you torne that relyke aboute
Other the trinite had the goute
Or elles bycause it is iii toes in one
God made it muche as thre toes alone

[PARDONER]

Well lette that passe and loke vpon thys
Here is a relyke that doth nat mys
To helpe the leste as well as the moste
This is a buttocke-bone of Pentecoste

POTYCARY

By chryste and yet for all your boste
Thys relyke hath be-shyten the roste

PARDONER

Marke well thys relyke here is a whipper
My friendes vnfayned here is a slypper

For by alhalowes me thynketh
That alhalowes breth stynketh
    palmer.
ye iudge alhalowes breth vnknowen
If any breth stynke it is your owne
    poticary.
I know myne own breth from alhalowes
Or els it were tyme to kysse the gallowes
    Pardoner.
Nay sirs beholde here may ye se
The great toe of the trinitie
Who to this toe any money voweth
And once may rolle it in his mouth
All his lyfe after I vndertake
He shalbe ryd of the tothake
    Poticarye.
I praye you tourne that relyke about
Other the trinitie had the goute
Or elle because it is thre toes in one
God made it muche as thre toes alone
    Pardoner.
Well let that passe and loke vpon this
Here is a relyke that doth not misse
To helpe the leaste aswell as the moste
This is a buttocke bone of penticost
    poticary.
By Chryste and yet for all your boste
This relyke hath beshypten the roste
    pardoner.
Marke well this relyke here is a whipper
My frinde vnfayned here is a slypper
Of one of the seuen slepers before
Doubtlesse this kysse shal do you great pleasure
For all these two dayes it shall so ease you
That none other sauours shall displease you
    poticarye.

All these two dayes, nay all these two yeare
For all the sauours that may come heare
Can be no worse for at a worde
One of the seuen slepers trode in a torde
    pedler.
Syr me thynketh your deuotion is but smal
    pardoner.
Smal, mary me thinketh he hath none at all
    poticarye.
What the Deuyll care I what ye thinke
Shall I prayse relikes when they stinke.
    pardoner.
Here is an eye toth of the great Turke
Whose eyes be ones set on this pece of worke
May happely lese part of his eye syght
But not all tyl he be blynde outryght.
    potycary.
What soeuer any other man seeth
I haue no deuocion to Turkes teeth
For although I neuer sawe a greater
Yet me thinketh I haue sene many beter
    prdoner.
Here is a boxe full of humble bees
That stonge Eue as she sat on her knees
Tastyng the frute to her forbidden
Who kisseth the bees within this hidden
Shall haue as muche pardon of ryght
As for anye relyke he kist thys nyght.
    palmer.
Syr I wyll kisse them with all my harte.
    potycary.
Kysse them agayne and take my part
For I am nat worthy, nay let be
Those bees that stonge Eue shall not sting me
    pardoner.
Good frendes I haue yet here in this glasse

A PAGE OF THE PLAY "THE FOURE P.P.," REPRODUCED ON P. 204 (OPPOSITE). [From another Edition of the Play]

Of one of the seuen slepers be sure
For all these two days do you great pleasure
For all these two days it shall so ease you
That none other sauours shall displease you

POTYCARY

All these two dayes nay all thys two yere
For all the sauours that may come here
Can be no worse for at a worde
One of the seuen slepers trode in a torde

PEDLER

Syr me thynketh your deuocion is but smal

PARDONER

Shall mary me thynketh he hath none at all

POTYCARY

What the deuyll care I what ye thynke
Shall I prayse relykes when they stynke

PARDONER

Here is an eye-toth of the great Turke
Whose eyes be ones sette on thys pece of worke
May happely lese parte of his eye-syght
But nat all tyll he be blynde out-ryght

POTYCARY

What-so-euer any other man seeth
I haue no deuacion to Turkes teeth
For all-though I neuer sawe a greter
Yet me thynketh I haue sene many better

PARDONER

Here is a box full of humble-bees
That stonge Eue as she sat on her knees

Tastynge the frute to her forbydden
Who kysseth the bees within this hydden
Shall haue as muche pardon of ryght
As for any relyke he kyst thys nyght

PALMER

Syr I wyll kysse them with all my herte

POTYCARY

Kysse them agayne and take my parte
For I am nat worthy nay lette be
Those bees that stonge Eue shall nat stynge me

PARDONER

Good frendes I haue yet[1] here in thys glas
Whiche on the drynke at the weddynge was
Of Adam and Eue vndoutedly
If ye honor this relyke deuoutly
All-though ye thurst no whyt the lesse
Ye shall ye drynke the more doutlesse
After whiche drynkynge ye shall be as mete
To stande on your hede as on your fete

POTYCARY

Ye mary now I can ye thanke
In presents of thys the reste be blanke
Wolde God this relyke had come rather
Kysse that relyke well good father
Suche is the payne that ye palmers take
To kysse the pardon-bowle for the drynke sake
O holy yeste that loketh full sowr and stale
For goddes body helpe me to a cuppe of ale
The more I be-holde the the more I thurste
The oftener I kysse the more lyke to burste

¹ = ye[s]t.

But syns I kysse the so deuoutely
Hyre me and helpe me with drynke till I dye
What so muche prayenge and so lytell spede

PARDONER

Ye for God knoweth whan it is nede
To sende folkes drynke but by saynt Antony
I wene he hath sent you to muche all-redy

POTYCARY

If I haue neuer the more for the
Then be the relykes no ryches to me
Nor to thy-selfe excepte they be
More benefycyall then I can se
Rycher is one boxe of [t]his tryacle
Then all thy relykes that do no myrakell
If thou haddest prayed but halfe so muche to me
As I haue prayed to thy relykes and the
Nothynge concernynge myne occupacion
But streyght shulde haue wrought in operacyon
And as in value I pas you an ace
Here lyeth muche rychesse in lytell space
I haue a boxe of rebarb here
Which is as deynty as it is dere
So helpe me god and hollydam
Of this I wolde nat geue a deam[1]
To the beste frende I haue in Englandes grounde
Though he wolde geue me xx pounde
For though the stomake do it abhor
It pourget[h] you clene from the color
And maketh your stomake sore to walter
That ye shall neuer come to the halter

----

[1] = dram.

PEDLER

Then is that medycyn a souerayn thynge
To preserue a man from hangynge

POTYCARY

If ye wyll taste but thys crome that ye se
If euer ye be hanged neuer truste me
Here haue I dispompholicus
A speciall oyntement as doctours discuse
For a fistela or a canker
Thys oyntement is euen shot-anker
For this medecyn helpeth one and other
Or bryngeth them in case that they nede no other
Here is syrapus de Byzansis
A lytell thynge is i-nough of this
For euen the weyght of one scryppull
Shall make you stronge as a cryppull
Here be other as diosfialios
Diagalanga and sticados
Blanka manna diospoliticon
Mercury sublyme and metridaticon
Pelitory and arsefetita
Cassy and colloquintita
These be the thynges that breke all stryfe
Betwene mannes sycknes and his lyfe
From all payne these shall you deleuer
And set you euen at reste for-euer
Here is a medecyn no mo lyke the same
Whiche comenly is called thus by name
Alikakabus or alkakengy
A goodly thynge for dogges that be mangy
Suche be these medycynes that I can
Helpe a dogge as well as a man
Nat one thynge here partycularly
But worketh vniuersally

o

For it doth me as muche good when I sell it
As all the byers that taste it or smell it
Now syns my medycyns be so specyall
And in operacion so generall
And redy to worke when-so-euer they shall
So that in ryches I am principall
If any rewarde may entreat ye
I besech you mashyp be good to me
And ye shall haue a boxe of marmelade
So fyne that ye may dyg it with a spade

PEDLER

Syr I thanke you but your rewarde
Is nat the thynge that I regarde
I muste and wyll be indifferent
Wherfore procede in your intente

POTYCARY

Nowe yf I wyst thys wysh no synne
I wolde to god I myght begynne

PARDONER

I am content that thou lye fyrste

PALMER

Euen so am I and say thy worste
Now let vs here of all thy lyes
The greatest lye thou mayst deuyse
And in the fewyst wordes thou can

POTYCARY

Forsoth ye be an honest man

PALMER

There sayde ye muche but yet no lye

PARDONER

Now lye ye bothe by our lady
Thou lyest in bost of hys honestie
And he hath lyed in affyrmynge the

POTYCARY

Yf we both lye and ye say true
Then of these lyes your parte adew
And yf ye wyn make none auaunt
For ye are sure of one yll seruaunte
Ye may perceyue by the wordes he gaue
He taketh your mashyp but for a knaue
But who tolde true or lyed in-dede
That wyll I knowe or we procede
Syr after that I fyrste began
To prayse you for an honest man
When ye affyrmed it for no lye
Now by our fayth speke euen truely
Thought ye your affyrmacion true

PALMER

Ye mary I for I wolde ye knewe
I thynke my-selfe an honest man

POTYCARY

What thought ye in the contrary than

PARDONER

In that I sayde the contrary
I thynke from trouth I dyd nat vary

POTYCARY

And what of my wordes

PARDONER

I thought ye lyed

POTYCARY

And so thought I by god that dyed
Nowe haue you twayne eche for hym-selfe layde
That none hath lyed out but both truesayd
And of vs twayne none hath denyed
But both affyrmed that I haue lyed
Now syns both your trouth confes
And that we both my lye so witnes
That twayne of vs thre in one agre
And that the lyer the wynner must be
Who coulde prouyde suche euydens
As I haue done in this pretens
Me thynketh this mater sufficient
To cause you to gyue iudgement
And to giue me the mastrye
For ye perceyue these knaues can nat lye

PALMER

Though nother of vs as yet had lyed
Yet what we can do is vntryed
For yet we haue deuysed nothynge
But answered you and geuen hyrynge

PEDLER

Therfore I haue deuysed one way
Wherby all thre your myndes may saye
For eche of you one tale shall tell
And whiche of you telleth most meruell
And most vnlyke to be true
Shall most preuayle what-euer-ensew

POTYCARY

If ye be set in mervalynge
Then shall ye here a meruaylouse thynge

And though in-dede all be nat true
Yet suer the most parte shall be new
I dyd a cure no lenger a-go
But Anno domini millesimo
On a woman yonge and so fayre
That neuer haue I sene a gayre
God saue all women from that lyknes
This wanton had the fallen-syknes
Whiche by dissent came lynyally
For her mother had it naturally
Wherfore this woman to recure
It was more harde ye may be sure
But though I boste my crafte is suche
That in suche thynges I can do muche
How ofte she fell were muche to reporte
But her hed so gydy and her helys so shorte
That with the twynglynge of an eye
Downe wolde she falle euyn by-and-by
But or she wolde aryse agayne
I shewed muche practyse muche to my payne
For the tallest man within this towne
Shulde nat with ease haue broken her sowne
All-though for lyfe I dyd nat doute her
Yet dyd I take more payne about her
Then I wolde take with my owne syster
Syr at the last I gaue her a glyster
I thrust a thampyon in her tewell
And bad her kepe it for a iewell
But I knewe it so heuy to cary
That I was sure it wolde nat tary
For where gonpouder is ones fyerd
The tampyon wyll no lenger be hyerd
Whiche was well sene in tyme of thys chaunce
For when I had charged this ordynaunce
Sodeynly as it had thonderd
Euen at a clap losed her bumberd

Now marke for here begynneth the reuell
This tampion flew x longe myle leuell
To a fayre castell of lyme and stone
For strength I knowe nat such a one
Whiche stode vpon an hyll full hye
At fote wherof a ryuer ranne bye
So depe tyll chaunce had it forbyden
Well myght the regent there haue ryden
But when this tampyon on this castell lyght
It put the castels so farre to flyght
That downe they came eche vpon other
No stone lefte standynge by goddes mother
But rolled downe so faste the hyll
In suche a nomber and so dyd fyll
From botom to bryme from shore to shore
Thys forsayd ryuer so depe before
That who lyste nowe to walke therto
May wade it ouer and wet no shoo
So was thys castell layd wyde open
That euery man myght se the token
But in a good hourse maye these wordes be spoken
After the tampyon on the walles was wroken
And pece by pece in peces broken
And she delyuered with suche violens
Of all her inconueniens
I lefte her in good helth and luste
And so she doth contynew I truste

·PEDLER

Syr in your cure I can nothynge tell
But to our purpose ye haue sayd well

PARDONER

Well syr then marke what I can say
I haue ben a pardoner many a day

And done greater cures gostely
Then euer he dyd bodely
Namely thys one whiche ye shall here
Of one departed within thys seuen yere
A frende of myne and lykewyse I
To her agayne was as frendly
Who fell so syke so sodeynly
That dede she was euen by-and-by
And neuer spake with preste nor clerke
Nor had no whyt of thys holy warke
For I was thens it coulde nat be
Yet harde I say she asked for me
And when I bethought me howe thys chaunced
And that I haue to heuen auaunced
So many soules to me but straungers
And coude nat kepe my frende from daungers
But she to dy so daungerously
For her soule helth especyally
That was the thynge that greued me soo
That nothynge coulde release my woo
Tyll I had tryed euen out of hande
In wat estate her soule dyd stande
For whiche tryall shorte tale to make
I toke thys iourney for her sake
Geue eare for here begynneth the story
From hens I went to purgatory
And toke with me thys gere in my fyste
Whereby I may do there what I lyste
I knocked and was let in quyckly
But lorde how lowe the soules made curtesy
And I to euery soule agayne
Dyd gyue a beck them to retayne
And axed them thys question than
Yf that the soule of suche a woman
Dyd late amonge them there appere

Wherto they sayd she came nat here
Then ferd I muche it was nat well
Alas thought I she is in hell
For with her lyfe I was so acqueynted
That sure I thought she was nat saynted
With thys it channced me to snese
Christe helpe   quoth a soule that ley for his fees
Those wordes quoth I thou shalt nat lees
Then with these pardons of all degrees
I payed hys tole and set hym so quyght
That strayt to heuen he toke his flyght
And I from thens to hell that nyght
To help this woman yf I myght
Nat as who sayth by authorite
But by the waye of entreate
And fyrst the deuyll that kept the gate
I came and spake after this rate
All hayle syr deuyll and made lowe curtesy
Welcome quoth he thys smillyngly
He knew me well and I at laste
Remembered hym syns longe tyme paste
For as good happe wolde haue it chaunce
Thys deuyll and I were of olde acqueyntaunce
For oft in the play of corpus Cristi
He had played the deuyll at Couentry
By his acqueyntaunce and my behauoure
He shewed to me ryght frendly fauoure
And to make my returne the shorter
I sayd to this deuyll Good mayster porter
For all olde loue yf it lye in your power
Helpe me to speke with my lorde and your
Be sure quoth he no tongue can tell
What tyme thou coudest haue come so well
For thys daye lucyfer fell
Whiche is our festyuall in hell

Nothynge vnreasonable craued thys day
That shall in hell haue any nay
But yet be-ware thou come nat in
Tyll tyme thou may thy pasporte wyn
Wherfore stande styll and I wyll wyt
If I can get thy saue-condyt
He taryed nat but shortely gat it
Under seale and the deuyls hande at it
In ample wyse as ye shall here
Thus it began Lucyfere
By the power of god cheyfe deuyll of hell
To all the deuyls that there do dwell
And euery of them we sende gretynge
Under streyght charge and commaundynge
That they aydynge and assystent be
To suche a pardoner and maned[1] me
So that he may at lybertie
Passe saue without hys ieopardy
Tyll that he be from vs extyncte
And clerely out of helles precincte
And hys pardons to kepe sauegarde
We wyll they lye in the porters warde
Geuyn in the fornes of our palys
In our hye courte of maters of malys
Suche a day and yere of our reyne
God saue the deuyll quoth I for playne
I truste thys wrytynge to be sure
Then put thy truste quoth he in euer
Syns thou art sure to take no harme
Thys deuyll and I walket arme in arme
So farre tyll he had brought me thyther
Where all the deuyls of hell togyther
Stode in a-ray in suche apparell
As for that day there metely fell

[1] = named.

Theyr hornes well gylt theyr clowes full clene
Theyr taylles well kempt and as I wene
With Sothery buttery theyr bodyes anoynted
I neuer sawe deuyls so well appoynted
The mayster deuyll sat in his iacket
And all the soules were playnge at racket
None other rackettes they hadde in hande
Saue euery soule a good fyre-brande
Wherwith they played so pretely
That Lucyfer laughed merely
And all the resedew of the f[r]endes
Dyd laugh full well togytther lyke frendes
But of my frende I saw no whyt
Nor durst nat axe for her as yet
Anone all this rout was brought in silens
And I by an vsher brought in presens
Then to Lucyfer low as I coude
I knelyd which he so well alowde
That thus he beckte and by saynt Antony
He smyled on me well-fauoredly
Bendynge hys browes as brode as barne-durres
Shakynge hys eares as ruged as burres
Rolynge hys yes as rounde as two bushels
Flastynge the fyre out of his nose-thryls
Gnashynge hys teeth so vayngloronsely
That me thought tyme to fall to flatery
Wherwith I tolde as I shall tell
O plesant pycture O prince of hell
Feurred in fashyon abominable
And syns that is inestimable
For me to prayse the worthyly
I leue of prays vnworthy
To geue the prays besechynge the
To heare my sewte and then to be
So good to graunt the thynge I craue
And to be shorte thys wolde I haue

The soule of one whiche hyther is flytted
Deliuered hens and to me remitted
And in thys doynge though al be nat quyt
Yet some parte I shall deserue it
As thus I am a pardoner
And ouer soules as a controller
Thorough-out the erth my power doth stande
Where many a soule lyeth on my hande
That spede in maters as I vse them
As I receyue them or refuse them
Wherby what tyme thy pleasure is
I shall requyre any part of thys
The leste deuyll here that can come thyther
Shall chose a soule and brynge hym hyther
Nowe quoth the deuyll we are well pleased
What is hys name thou woldest haue eased
Nay quoth I be it good or euyll
My comynge is for a she-deuyll
What calste her quoth he thou horyson
Forsoth quoth I Margery coorson
Now by our honour sayd Lucyfer
No deuyll in hell shall witholde her
And yf thou woldest haue twenty mo
Were nat for iustyce they shulde goo
For all we deuyls within thys den
Haue more to do with two women
Then with all the charge we haue besyde
Wherfore yf thou our frende wyll be tryed
Aply thy pardons to women so
That vnto vs there come no mo
To do my beste I promysed by othe
Which I haue kepte for as the fayth goth
At thys dayes to heuen I do procure
Ten women to one man be sure
Then of Lucyfer my leue I toke
And streyght vnto the mayster coke

I was hadde into the kechyn
For Margaryes offyce was ther-in
All thynge handled there discretely
For euery soule bereth offyce metely
Which myght be sene to se her syt
So bysely turnynge of the spyt
For many a spyt here hath she turned
And many a good spyt hath she burned
And many a spyt full hoth hath tosted
Before the meat coulde be halfe rosted
And or the meate were half rosted in-dede
I toke her then fro the spyt for spede
But when she saw thys brought to pas
To tell the ioy wherin she was
And of all the deuyls for ioy how they
Dyd rore at her delyuery
And how the cheynes in hell dyd rynge
And how all the soules therin dyd synge
And how we were brought to the gate
And how we toke our leue therat
Be suer lacke of tyme sufferyth nat
To reherse the xx parte of that
Wherfore thys tale to conclude breuely
Thys woman thanked me chyefly
That she was ryd of thys endles deth
And so we departed on new-marked heth
And yf that any man do mynde her
Who lyste to seke her there shall he fynde her

PEDLER

Syr ye haue sought her wonders well
And where ye founde her as ye tell
To here the chaunce ye founde in hell
I fynde ye were in great parell

PALMER

His tale is all muche parellous
But parte is muche more meruaylous
As where he sayde the deuyls complayne
That women put them to suche payne
By theyr condicions so croked and crabbed
Frowardly fashonde so waywarde and wrabbed
So farre in deuision and sturrynge suche stryfe
That all the deuyls be wery of theyr lyfe
This in effect he tolde for trueth
Whereby muche muruell to me ensueth
That women in hell suche shrewes can be
And here so gentyll as farre as I se
Yet haue I sene many a myle
And many a woman in the whyle
Nat one good cytye towne nor borough
In cristendom but I haue ben through
And this I wolde ye shulde vnderstande
I haue sene women v hundred thousande

*   *   *   *   *

And oft with them haue longe tyme maryed
Yet in all places where I haue ben
Of all the women that I haue sene
I neuer sawe nor knewe in my consyens
Any one woman out of paciens

POTYCARY

By the masse there is a great lye

PARDONER

I neuer harde a greater by our lady

PEDLER

A greater nay know ye any so great

PALMER
Syr whether that I lose or get
For my parte iudgement shall be prayed

PARDONER
And I desyer as he hath sayd

POTYCARY
Procede and ye shall be obeyed

PEDLER
Then shall nat iudgement be delayd
Of all these thre yf eche mannes tale
In Poules churche-yarde were set on sale
In some mannes hande that hath the sleyghte
He shulde sure sell these tales by weyght
For as they wey so be they worth
But whiche weyth beste to that now forth
Syr all the tale that ye dyd tell
I bere in mynde and yours as well
And as ye sawe the mater metely
So lyed ye bothe well and discretely
Yet were your lyes with the lest truste me
For yf ye had sayd ye had made fle
Ten tampyons out of ten womens tayles
Ten tymes ten myle to ten castels or iayles
And fyll ten ryuers ten tymes so depe
As ten of that whiche your castell stones dyde kepe
Or yf te ten tymes had bodely
Fet ten soules out of purgatory
And ten tymes so many out of hell
Yet by these ten bonnes I could ryght well
Ten tymes sonner all that haue beleued
Then the tenth parte of that he hath meued

POTYCARY

Two knaues before i lacketh ii knaues of fyue
Then one and then one and bothe knaues a-lyue
Then two and then two and thre at a cast
Thou knaue and thou knaue and thou knaue at laste
Nay knaue yf ye try me by nomber
I wyll as knauyshly you accomber
Your mynde is all on your pryuy tythe
For all in ten me thynketh your wit lythe
Now ten tymes I beseche hym that hye syttes
Thy wyfes x cōmaūdementes may serch thy v wittes
Then ten of my tordes in ten of thy teth
And ten of thy nose whiche euery man seth
And twenty tymes ten this wyshe I wolde
That thou haddest ben hanged at ten yere olde
For thou goest about to make me a slaue
I wyll thou knowe yf I am a gentylman knaue
And here is an other shall take my parte

PARDONER

Nay fyrste I be-shrew your knaues herte
Or I take parte in your knauery
I wyll speke fayre by one lady[1]
Syr I beseche your mashyp to be
As good as ye can be to me

PEDLER

I wolde be glade to do you good
And hym also be he neuer so wood
But dout you nat I wyll now do
The thynge my consciens ledeth me to
Both your tales I take farre impossyble
Yet take I his father[2] incredyble

---

[1] = our Lady.   [2] = farther

Nat only the thynge it-selfe alloweth it
But also the boldenes therof auoweth it
I knowe nat where your tale to trye
Nor yours but in hell or purgatorye
But hys boldnes hath faced a lye
That may be tryed euyn in thys compayne
As yf ye lyste to take thys order
Amonge the women in thys border
Take thre of the yongest and thre of the oldest
Thre of the hotest and thre of the coldest
Thre of the wysest and thre of the shrewdest
Thre of the chastest and thre of the lewdest
Thre of the lowest and thre of the hyest
Thre of the farthest and thre of the nyest
Thre of the fayrest and thre of the maddest
Thre of the fowlest and thre of the saddest
And when all these threes be had a-sonder
Of eche thre two iustly by nomber
Shall be founde shrewes excepte thys fall
That ye hap to fynde them shrewes all
Hym-selfe for trouth all this doth knowe
And oft hath tryed some of thys rowe
And yet he swereth by his consciens
He neuer saw woman breke paciens
Wherfore consydered with true entente
Hys lye to be so euident
And to appere so euydently
That both you affyrmed it a ly
And that my consciens so depely
So depe hath sought thys thynge to try
And tryed it with mynde indyfferent
Thus I awarde by way of iudgement
Of all the lyes ye all haue spent
Hys lye to be most excellent

PALMER

Syr though ye were bounde of equyte
To do as ye haue done to me
Yet do I thanks you of your payne
And wyll requyte some parte agayne

PARDONER

Mary syr ye can no les do
But thanke hym as muche as it cometh to
And so wyll I do for my parte
Now a vengeaunce on thy knaues harte
I neuer knewe pedler a iudge before
Nor neuer wyll truste pedlynge-knaue more
What doest thou there thou horson nody

POTYCARY

By the masse lerne to make curtesy
Curtesy before and curtesy behynde hym
And then on eche syde the deuyll blynde hym
Nay when I haue it perfytly
Ye shall haue the deuyll and all of curtesy
But it is nat sone lerned brother
One knaue to make curtesy to another
Yet when I am angry that is the worste
I shall call my mayster knaue at the fyrste

PALMER

Then wolde some mayster perhappes clowt ye
But as for me ye nede nat doute ye
For I had leuer be without ye
Then haue suche besynesse aboute ye

PARDONER

So helpe me god so were ye better
What shulde a begger be a ietter

P

It were no whyt your honestie
To haue vs twayne iet after ye

POTYCARY

Syr be ye sure he telleth you true
Yf we shulde wayte thys wolde ensew
It wolde be sayd truste me at a worde
Two knaues made curtesy to a thyrde

PEDLER

Now by my trouth to speke my mynde
Syns they be so loth to be assyned
To let them lose I thynke it beste
And so shall ye lyue beste in rest

PALMER

Syr I am nat on them so fonde
To compell them to kepe theyr bonde
And syns ye lyste nat to wayte on me
I clerely of waytynge dyscharge ye

PARDONER

Mary syr I hertely thanke you

POTYCARY

And I lyke-wyse I make god auowe

PEDLER

Now be ye all euyn as ye begoon
No man hath loste nor no man hath woon
Yet in the debate wherwith ye began
By waye of aduyse I wyll speke as I can
I do perceyue that pylgrymage
Is chyeyfe the thynge ye haue in vsage

Wherto in effecte for loue of Chryst
Ye haue or shulde haue bene entyst
And who so doth with suche entent
Doth well declare hys tyme well spent
And so do ye in your pretence
If ye procure thus indulgence
Unto your neyghbours charytably
For loue of them in god onely
All thys may be ryght well applyed
To shewell you both well occupyed
For though ye walke nat bothe one waye
Yet walkynge thus thys dare I saye
That bothe your walkes come to one ende
And so for all that do pretende
By ayde of Goddes grace to ensewe
Any maner kynde of vertue
As some great almyse for to gyue
Some in wyllfull pouertie to lyue
Some to make hye-wayes and suche other warkes
And some to mayntayne prestes and clarkes
To synge and praye for soule[s] departed
These with all other vertues well marked
All-though they be of sondry kyndes
Yet be they nat vsed with sondry myndes
But as god only doth all those moue
So euery man onely for his loue
With loue and dred obediently
Worketh in these vertues vnyformely
Thus euery vertue yf we lyste to scan
Is pleasaunt to god and thankfull to man
And who that by grace of the holy goste
To any one vertue is moued moste
That man by that grace that one apply
And therin serue god most plentyfully
Yet nat that one so farre wyde to wreste

So lykynge the same to myslyke the reste
For who so wresteth hys worke is in vayne
And euen in that case I perceyue you twayne
Lykynge your vertue in suche wyse
That eche others vertue you to dyspyse
Who walketh thys way for god wolde fynde hyn
The farther they seke hym the farther behynde hym
One kynde of vertue to dyspyse another
Is lyke as the syster myght hange the brother

POTYCARY

For fere lest suche parels to me myght fall
I thanke god I vse no vertue at all

PEDLER

That is of all the very worste waye
For more harde it is as I haue harde saye
To begynne vertue where none is pretendyd
Then where it is begonne the abuse to be mended
How-be-it ye be nat all to begynne
One syne of vertue ye are entred in
As thys I suppose ye dyd saye true
In that ye sayd ye vse no vertue
In the whiche wordes I dare well reporte
Ye are well be-loued of all thys sorte
By your raylynge here openly
At pardons ond relyques so leudly

POTYCARY

In that I thynke my faute nat great
For all that he hath I knowe conterfete

PEDLER

For his and all other that ye knowe fayned
Ye be nother counceled nor constrayned

To any suche thynge in any suche case
To gyue any reuerence in any suche place
But where ye dout the truthe nat knowynge
Beleuynge the beste good may be growynge
In iudgynge the beste no harme at the leste
In iudgynge the worste no good at the beste
But beste in these thynges it semeth to me
To take no iudgement vpon ye
But as the churche doth iudge or take them
So do ye receyue or forsake them
And so be sure ye can nat erre
But may be a frutfull folower

POTYCARY

Go ye before and as I am true man
I wyll folow as faste as I can

PARDONER

And so wyll I for he hath sayd so well
Reason wolde we shulde folowe hys counsell

PALMER

Then to our reason god gyue vs his grace
That we may folowe with fayth so fermely
His commaundementes that we may purchace
His loue and so consequently
To byleue hys churche faste and faythfully
So that we may accordynge to his promyse
Be kept out of errour in any wyse
And all that hath scapet vs here by neglygence
We clerely reuoke and forsake it
To passe the tyme in thys without offence
Was the cause why the maker dyd make it
And so we humbly beseche you take it

Besechynge our lorde to prosper you all
In the fayth of hys churche uniuersall

FINIS

Imprynted at London in Fletestrete
at the sygne of the George by
Wyllyam Myddylton

JOHAN JOHAN

FROM THE COPY IN THE PEPYS COLLECTION
MAGDALENE COLLEGE, CAMBRIDGE; EDITION 1533.

THE ONLY OTHER COPY KNOWN IS IN THE BODLEIAN.

JOHAN JOHAN

A MERY PLAY

betwene John Johan the
husbande Tyb his
wyfe and syr Jhān
the preest

JOHAN JOHAN THE HUSBANDE

God spede you maysters euerychone
Wote ye not whyther my wyfe is gone
I pray god the dyuell take her
For all that I do I can not make her
But she wyll go a gaddynge very myche
Lyke an Anthony pyg with an olde wyche
Whiche ledeth her abouth hyther and thyther
But by our lady I wote not whyther
But by gogges blod were she come home
Vnto this my house by our lady of crome
I wolde bete her or that I drynke
Bete her q[uo]d a   yea that she shall stynke
And at euery stroke lay her on the grounde
And trayne her by the here abouth the house rounde
I am euyn mad that I bete her not nowe
But I shall rewarde her hardly well ynowe
There is neuer a wyfe betwene heuen and hell
Whiche was euer beten halfe so well
    Beter q[uo]d a   yea but what and she thereof dye
Than I may chaunce to be hanged shortly
And whan I haue beten her tyll she smoke
And gyuen her many a C stroke
Thynke ye that she wyll amende yet
Nay by our lady the deuyll spede whyt
Therefore I wyll not bete her at all
    And shall I not bete her no shall

When she offendeth and doth amys
And kepeth not her house as her duetie is
Shall I not bete her if she do so
Yes by cokkes blood that shall I do
I shall bete her and thwak her I trow
That she shall beshyte the house for very wo
    But yet I thynk what my neybour wyll say than
He wyll say thus whom chydest y[ou] Johan Johan
Mary wyll I say I chyde my curst wyfe
The veryest drab that euer bare lyfe
Whiche doth nothyng but go and come
And I can not make her kepe her at home
Than I thynke he wyll say by and by
Walke her cote Johan Johan and bete her hardely
But than vnto hym myn answer shalbe
The more I bete her the worse is she
And wors and wors make her I shall
    He wyll say than bete her not at all
And why shall I say this wolde be wyst
Is she not myne to chastice as I lyst
    But this is another poynt worst of all
The folkes wyll mocke me whan they here me brall
But for all that shall I let therefore
To chastyce my wife euer the more
And to make her at home for to tary
Is not that well done yes by saynt mary
That is a poynt of an honest man
For to bete his wyfe well nowe and than
    Therfore I shall bete her haue ye no drede
And I ought to bete her tyll she be starke dede
And why by god bicause it is my pleasure
And if I shulde suffre her I make you sure
Nought shulde p̄uayle[1] me nother staffe nor waster
Within a whyle she wolde be my mayster

             [1] = p[re]uayle.

Therfore I shall bete her by cokkes mother
Both on the tone side and on the tother
Before and behynde nought shall be her bote
From the top of the head to the sole of the fote
But masters for goddes sake do not entrete
For her whan that she shalbe bete
But for goddes passion let me alone
And I shall thwak her that she shall grone
Wherfore I beseche you and hartely you pray
And I beseche you say me not nay
But that I may beate her for this ones
And I shall beate her by cokkes bones
That she shall stynke lyke a pole kat
But yet by gogges body that nede nat
For she wyll stynke without any betyng
For euery nyght ones she gyueth me an hetyng
From her issueth suche a stynkyng smoke
That the sauour therof almost doth me choke
But I shall bete her nowe without fayle
I shall bete her toppe and tayle
Heed shulders armes legges and all
I shall bete her I trowe that I shall
And by gogges boddy I tell you trewe
I shall bete her tyll she be blacke and blewe
But where the dyuell trowe ye she is gon
I holde a noble she is with syr Johan
I fere I am begyled alway
But yet in fayth I hope well nay
Yet I almost enrage that I ne can
Se the behauour of our gentylwoman
And yet I thynke thyther as she doth go
Many an honest wyfe goth thyther also
For to make some pastyme and sporte
But than my wyfe so ofte doth thyther resorte
That I fere she wyll make me weare a fether

But yet I nede not for to fere nether
For he is her gossyp that is he
 But abyde a whyle yet let me se
Where the dyuell hath our gossypry begon
My wyfe had neuer chylde doughter nor son
 Howe if I forbede her that she go no more
Yet wyll she go as she dyd before
Or els wyll she chuse some other place
And then the matter is in as yll case
 But in fayth all these wordes be in wast
For I thynke the matter is done and past
And whan she cometh home she wyll begyn to chyde
But she shall haue her payment styk by her syde
For I shall order her for all her brawlyng
That she shall repent to go a catter wawlyng

[TYB]
Why whom wylt thou beate I say thou knaue

JHĀN
Who I tyb none so god me saue

TYB
Yes I harde the say thou woldest one bete

JHĀN
Mary wyfe it was stokfysshe in temmes strete
Whiche wyll be good meate agaynst lent
Why tyb what haddest y[ou] thought yt I had ment

TYB.
Mary me thought I harde the bawlyng
Wylt thou neuer leue this wawlyng
Howe the dyuell dost thou thy selfe behaue
Shall we euer haue this worke thou knaue

JHĀN

What wyfe howe sayst y[ou] was it well gest of me
That thou woldest be come home in safete
Assone as I had kendled a fyre
Come warme the swete tyb I the requyre

TYB.

O Johan Johan I am afrayd by this lyght
That I shalbe sore syk this night

JHĀN

By cokkes soule now I dare lay a swan
That she comes nowe streyght fro syr Johan
For euer whan she hath fatched of hym a lyk
Than she comes home and sayth she is syk

TYB.

What sayst thou.

J.

Mary I say
It is mete for a woman to go play
Abrode in the towne for an houre or two

TYB.

Well gentylman go to go to

JHĀN

Well let vs haue no more debate

TYB.

If he do not fyght chyde and rate
Braule and fare as one that were frantyke
There is nothyng that may hym lyke

JHĀN

If that the parysshe preest syr Johan
Dyd not se her nowe and than
And gyue her absolution vpon a bed
For wo and payne she wolde sone be deed

TYB.

For goddes sake Jhān Johan do the most displease
Many a tyme I am yll at ease
What thynkest nowe am not I somwhat syk

JHĀN

Nowe wolde to god and swete saynt Dyryk
That thou warte in the water vp to the throte
Or in a burnyng ouen red hote
To se and I wolde pull the out

TYB

Nowe Johan Johan to put the out of dout
Imagyn thou where that I was
Before I cam home

J.
My pcase
Thou wast prayenge in the churche of poules
Vpon thy knees for all chrysten soules

TYB

Nay

J.
Than if thou wast not so holy
Shewe me where thou wast and make no lye

TYB

Truely Johan Johan we made a pye
I and my gossyp Margery

And our gossyp the preest syr Johan
And my neybours yongest doughter An
The preest payde for the stuffe and the makyng
And Margery she payde for the bakyng

JHĀN
By kokkes lylly woundes that same is she
That is the most bawde hens to Couentre

TYB.
What say you

J.
Mary answere me to this
Is not syr Johan a good man

TYB.
Yes that he is

JHĀN
Ha Tyb if I shulde not greue the
I haue somwhat wheref I wolde meue the

TYB.
Well husbande nowe I do coniect
That thou hast me somwhat in suspect
But by my soule I neuer go to syr Johan
But I fynde hym lyke an holy man
For eyther he is sayenge his deuotion
Or els he is goynge in p̄cessyon[1]

JHĀN
Yea rounde about the bed doth he go
You two to gether and no mo
And for to fynysshe the p̄cessyon[1]
He lepeth vp and thou lyest downe

[1] = p[ro]cessyon.

TYB.

What sayst thou

J.

Mary I say he doth well
For so ought a shepherde to do as I harde tell
For the saluation of all his folde

TYB.

Johan Johan

[J.]

What is it that thou wolde

TYB.

By my soule I loue the too too
And I shall tell the or I further go
The pye that was made I haue it nowe here
And therwith I trust he shall make good chere

JHĀN

By kokkes body that is very happy

TYB.

But wotest who gaue it

J.

What ye dyuel rek I

TYB.

By my fayth and I shall say trewe than
The dyuell take me and it were not syr Johan

Wold gyue me no meate/for my suffraunce
Vp kokes soule I wyll take no lenger payn
Ye shall do all your self/with a very vengeaunce
For me/and take thou there thy payle now
And yf thou canst mend it let me se how

Tyb. A horson knaue hast thou brok my payll
Thou shalt repent/by kokes lylly nayll
Rech me my dystaf/or my clyppyng sherre
I shall make the blood ronne about his erys

Johan. Nay stand styll dyab/I say and come no nere
For by kokes blood/yf thou come here
Or yf thou onys styr/toward this place
I shall throw this shoupll full of colys in thy face

Tyb. Ye horson dryuyll/get the out of my dore
Johan. Nay get thy out of my house/thou prest hore
Sir I. Thou lyest horson kokold/euyn to thy face
Johan. And thou lyest ppyld prest/with an euyll grace
Tyb. And y lyest I. Ca y lyest.sir. Ca y lyest agayn
Johan. Vp kokes soule horson prest/thou shalt be slayn
Thou hast eate our ppe/and gyue me nonght
Vp kokes blod it shalbe full derely bought

Tyb. At hym syr Johan/or els god gyue the sorow
Johan. Ca haue at your hore a these/sayint george to boro
Here they fyght by the erys a whyle a than
the prest and the wyfe go out of the place.

Johan. A syrs I haue payd some of them euen as I lyst
They haue borne/many a blow with my fyst
I thank god/I haue walkyd them well
And dryuen them hene/but yet can ye tell
Whether they be go/for by god I fere me
That they be gon together he and she
Vnto his chamber/and perhappys she wyll
Spyte of my hart/tary there styll
And peraduenture/there he and she
Wyll make me kokold/euyn to anger me
And then had I a pyg in the worse panyer
Therfore by god/I wyll hye me thyder
To se yf they do me any vylany
And thus fare well this noble company.
Finis.

Imprynted by Wyllyam Rastell/the .xii.day of
februarp the yere of our lord.M.ccccc.and.xxxiii,
Cum priuilegio.

THE LAST PAGE OF "JOHAN JOHAN"

(See pages 266 and 267)

JHĀN

O holde the peas wyfe and swere no more
But I beshrewe both your hartes therfore

TYB.

Yet peradventure thou hast suspection
Of that that was neuer thought nor done

[JHĀN]

Tusshe wyfe let all suche matters be
I loue the well though thou loue not me
But this pye doth nowe catche harme
Let vs set it vpon the harth to warme

TYB.

Than let vs eate it as fast as we can
But bycause syr Johan is so honest a man
I wolde that he shulde therof eate his part

JHĀN

That were reason I the ensure

TYB.

Than syns that it is thy pleasure
I pray the than go to hym ryght
And pray hym come sup with vs to nyght

JHĀN

Shall he cū hyther by kokkes soule I was a curst
Whan that I graunted to that worde furst
But syns I haue sayd it I dare not say nay
For than my wyfe and I shulde make a fray
But whan he is come I swere by goddes mother
I wold gyue the dyuell ye tone to cary away ye tother

TYB.

What sayst

JO.

Mary he is my curate I say
My confessour and my frende alway
Therfore go thou and seke hym by and by
And tyll thou come agayne I wyll kepe the pye

TYB.

Shall I go for hym nay I shrewe me than
Go thou and seke as fast as thou can
And tell hym it

J.

Shall I do so
In fayth it is not mete for me to go

TYB.

But thou shalte go tell hym for all that

JHĀN

Than shall I tell hym wotest what
That thou desyrest hym to come make some chere

TYB.

Nay that thou desyrest hym to come sup here

JHĀN

Nay by the rode wyfe y[ou] shalt haue the worshyp
And the thankes of thy gest that is thy gossyp

TYB.

Full ofte I se my husbande wyll me rate
For this hether commyng of our gentyll curate

JHĀN

What sayst Tyb let me here that agayne

TYB.

Mary I perceyue very playne
That thou hast syr Johan somwhat in suspect
But by my soule as far as I coniect
He is vertuouse and full of charyte

JHĀN

In fayth all the towne knoweth better than he
Is a hore monger a haunter of the stewes
An ypocrite a knaue that all men refuse
A lyer a wretche a maker of stryfe
Better than they knowe that thou art my good wyfe

TYB.

What is that that thou hast sayde

JHĀN

Mary I wolde have the table set and layde
In this place or that I care nor whether

TYB.

Than go to brynge the trestels hyther
Abyde a whyle let me put of my gown
But yet I am afrayde to lay it down
For I fere It shalbe sone stolen

[JHĀN]

And yet it may lye safe ynough vnstolen

[TYB.]

It may lye well here and I lyst
But by cokkes soule here hath a dogge pyst

And if I shulde lay it on the harth bare
It myght hap to be burned or I were ware
Therfore I pray you take ye the payne
To kepe my gowne tyll I come agayne
But yet he shall not haue it by my fay
He is so nere the dore he myght ron away
But bycause that ye be trusty and sure
Ye shall kepe it and it be your pleasure
And bycause it is arayde at the skyrt
Whyle ye do nothyng skrape of the durt

[JHĀN]
Lo nowe am I redy to go to syr Johan
And byd hym come as fast as he can

[TYB.]
Ye do so without ony taryeng
But I say harke thou hast forgot one thyng
Set vp the table and that by and by
Nowe go thy ways

J.
I go shortly
But se your candelstykkes be not out of the way

TYB.
Come agayne and lay the table I say
What me thynkes ye haue sone don

JHĀN.
Nowe I pray god that his malediction
Lyght on my wyfe and on the baulde preest

TYB.
Nowe go thy ways and hye the seest

JHĀN

I pray to Christ if my wyshe be no synne
That ye preest may breke his neck whan he comes in

TYB.

How cū agayn

J.

What a myschefe wylt y[ou] fole

TYB.

Mary I say brynge hether yender stole

JHĀN.

Nowe go to a lyttell wolde make me
For to say thus a vengaunce take the

TYB.

Nowe go to hym and tell hym playn
That tyll thou brynge hym y[ou] wylt not come agayn

JHĀN.

This pye doth borne here as it doth stande

TYB.

Go washe me these two cuppes in my hande

JHĀN.

I go with a myschyefe lyght on thy face

TYB.

Go and byd hym hye hym a pace
And the whyle I shall all thynges amende

JHĀN.

This pye burneth here at this ende
Vnderstandest thou

T.

Go thy ways I say

JHĀN.

I wyll go nowe as fast as I may

TYB.

Now come ones agayne I had forgot
Loke and there be ony ale in the pot

JHĀN.

Nowe a vengaunce and a very myschyefe
Lyght on the pylde preest and on my wyfe
On the pot the ale and on the table
The candyll the pye and all the rable
On the trystels and on the stole
It is moche ado to please a curst fole

TYB.

Go thy ways nowe and tary no more
For I am a hungred very sore

JHĀN.

Mary I go

T.

But come ones agayne yet
Brynge hyther that breade lest I forget it

JHĀN.

I wys it were tyme for to torne
The pye for ywys it doth borne

TYB.

Lorde howe my husbande nowe doth patter
And of the pye styl doth clatter
Go nowe and byd hym come away
I haue byd the an hundred tymes to day

JHĀN.

I wyll not gyue a strawe I tell you playne
If that the pye waxe colde agayne

TYB.

What art thou not gone yet out of this place
I had went thou haddest ben come agayne in ye space
But by cokkes soule and I shulde do the ryght
I shulde breke thy knaues heed to nyght

JHĀN.

Nay than if my wyfe be set a chydyng
It is tyme for me to go at her byddyng
There is a prouerbe whiche trewe nowe preueth
He must nedes go that the dyuell dryueth

How mayster curate may I come in
At your chamber dore without ony syn

SYR JOHAN THE PREEST.

Who is there nowe that wolde haue me
What Johan Johan what newes with the

JHĀN.

Mary syr to tell you shortly
My wyfe and I pray you hartely
And eke desyre you with all our myght
That ye wolde come and sup with vs to nyght

SYR J.

Ye must pardon me in fayth I ne can

JHĀN.

Yes I desyre you good syr Johan
Take payne this ones and yet at the lest
If ye wyll do nought at my request
Yet do somwhat for the loue of my wyfe

SYR J.

I wyll not go for makyng of stryfe
But I shall tell the what thou shalte do
Thou shalt tary and sup with me or thou go

JHĀN.

Wyll ye not go than why so
I pray you tell me is there ony dysdayne
Or ony enmyte betwene you twayne

SYR J.

In fayth to tell the betwene the and me
She is as wyse a woman as any may be
I know it well for I haue had the charge
Of her soule and serchyd her conscyens at large
I neuer knew her but honest and wyse
Without any yuyll[1] or any vyce   •
Saue one faut I know in her no more
And because I rebuke her now and then therfore
She is angre with me and hath me in hate
And yet that that I do I it for your welth

JHĀN.

Now god yeld it yow god master curate
And as ye do so send you your helth
Ywys I am bound to you a plesure

¹ = evil.

SYR J.

Yet thou thynkyst amys peraduenture
That of her body she shuld not be a good woman
But I shall tell the what I haue done Johan
For that matter she and I be somtyme aloft
And I do lye vppon her many a tyme and oft
To proue her yet could I neuer espy
That euer any dyd wors with her than I

JHĀN.

Syr that is the lest care I haue of nyne
Thankyd be god and your good doctryne
But yf it please you tell me the matter
And the debate betwene you and her

SYR J.

I shall tell the but thou must kepe secret

JHĀN.

As for that syr I shall not let

SYR J.

I shall tell the now the matter playn
She is angry with me and hath me in dysdayn
Because that I do her oft intyce
To do some penaunce after myne aduyse
Because she wyll neuer leue her wrawlyng
But alway with the she is chydyng and brawlyng
And therfore I knowe she hatyth me presens

JHĀN.

Nay in good feyth sauyng your reuerens

SYR J.

I know very well she hath me in hate

JHĀN.

Nay I dare swere for her master curate
But was I not a very knaue
I thought surely so god me saue
That he had louyd my wyfe for to dyseyue me
And now he quytyth hym self and here I se
He doth as much as he may for his lyfe
To stynk¹ the debate betwene my and my wyfe

SYR J.

If euer she dyd or though me any yll.
Now I forgyue her with me fre wyll
Therfor Johan Johan now get the home
And thank thy wyfe and say I wyll not come

JHĀN.

Yet let me know now good syr Johan
Where ye wyll go to supper than

SYR J.

I care nat greatly and I tell the
On saterday last I and .ii. or thre
Of my frendes made an appoyntement
And agaynst this nyght we dyd assent
That in a place we wolde sup together
And one of them sayd he wolde brynge thether
Ale and bread and for my parte I
Sayd that I wolde gyue them a pye
And there I gaue them money for the makynge
And an other sayd she wolde pay for the bakyng
And so we purpose to make good chere
For to dryue away care and thought

¹ = stynt.

JHĀN.

Than I pray you syr tell me here
Whyther shulde all this geare be brought

SYR J.

By my fayth and I shulde not lye
It shulde be delyuered to thy wyfe the pye

JHĀN.

By god it is at my house standyng by the fyre

SYR J.

Who bespake that pye I the requyre

JHĀN.

By my feyth and I shall not lye
It was my wyfe and her gossyp Margerye
And your good masshyp called syr Johan
And my newbours yongest doughter An
Your masshyp payde for the stuffe and makyng
And Margery she payde for the bakyng

SYR J.

If thou wylte haue me nowe in faithe I wyll go

JHĀN.

Ye mary I beseche your masshyp do so
My wyfe taryeth for none but vs twayne
She thynketh longe or I come agayne

SYR J.

Well nowe if she chyde me in thy presens
I wylbe content and take in pacyens

JHĀN.

By cokkes soule and she ones chyde
Or frowne or loure or loke asyde
I shall brynge you a staffe as myche as I may heue
Than bete her and spare not I gyue you good leue
To chastyce her for her shreude varyeng

TYB.

The deuyll take the for thy longe taryeng
·Here is not a whyt of water by my gowne
To washe our handes that we myght syt downe
Go and hye the as fast as a snayle
And with fayre water fyll me this payle

JHĀN.

I thanke our lorde of his good grace
That I can not rest longe in a place

TYB.

Go fetche water I say at a worde
For it is tyme the pye were on the borde
And go with a vengeaunce and say thou art prayde

SYR J.

A good gossyp is that well sayde

TYB.

Welcome myn owne swete harte
We shall make some chere or we departe

JHĀN.

Cokkes soule loke howe he approcheth nere
Vnto my wyfe this abateth my chere

SYR J.

By god I wolde ye had harde the tryfyls
The toys the mokkes the fables and the nyfyls
That I made thy husbāde to beleue and thynke
Thou myghtest as well in to the erthe synke
As thou coudest forbeare laughyng any whyle

TYB.

I pray the let me here parte of that wyle

SYR J.

Mary I shall tell the as fast as I can
But peas no more yonder cometh thy good man

JHĀN.

Cokkes soule what haue we here
As far as I sawe he drewe very nere
Vnto my wyfe

T.

What art come so sone
Gyue vs water to wasshe nowe haue done

Than he bryngeth the payle empty

JHĀN.

By kockes soule it was euen nowe full to ye brynk
But it was out agayne or I coude thynke
Wherof I marueled by god almyght
And than I loked betwene me and the lyght
As I spyed a clyfte bothe large and wyde
Lo wyfe here it is on the tone syde

TYB.

Why dost not stop it.

J.
Why howe shall I do it

TYB.

Take a lytle wax

J.
Howe shal I come to it

SYR. J.
Mary here be .ii. wax candyls I say
Whiche my gossyp margery gaue me yesterday

TYB.
Tusshe let hym alone for by the rode
It is pyte to helpe hym or do hym good

SYR. J.
What Jhān Jhān canst thou make no shyfte
Take this waxe as stop therwith the clyfte

JHĀN.
This waxe is as harde as any wyre

TYB.
Thou must chafe it a lytle at the fyre

JHĀN.
She yt brought the these waxe candelles twayne
She is a good companyon certayn

TYB.
What was it not my gossyp margery

SYR. J.
Yes she is a blessed woman surely

TYB.

Nowe wolde god I were as good as she
For she is vertuous and full of charyte

JHĀN.

Nowe so god helpe me and by my holydome ·
She is the erranst baud betwene this and Rome

TYB.

· What sayst

JHĀN
Mary I chafe the wax
And I chafe it so hard that my fyngers brakkes
But take vp this py that I here torne
And it stand long ywys it wyll borne

TYB.

Je but thou must chefe the wax I say

JHĀN.

Bid hym syt down I the pray
Syt down good syr Johan I you requyre

TYB.

Go. I say and chafe the wax by the fyre
Whyle that we sup syr Jhān and I

JHĀN.

And how now what wyll ye do with the py
Shall I not ete therof a morsell

TYB.

Go and chafe the wax whyle thou art well
And let vs haue no more pratyng thus

SYR. J.

Benedicite

J.

Dominus

TYB.

Now go chafe the wax with a myschyfe

JHĀN.

What I come to blysse the bord swete wyfe
It is my custome now and than
Mych good do it you master syr Jhān

TYB.

Go chafe the wax and here no lenger tary

JHĀN.

And is not this a very purgatory
To se folkes ete and may not ete a byt
By kokkes soule I am a very wodcok
This payle here now a vengaunce take it
Now my wyfe gyveth me a proud mok

TYB.

What dost

J.

Mary I chafe the waxe here
And I ymagyn to make you good chere
That a vengaunce take you both as ye syt
For I know well I shall not ete a byt
But yet in feyth yf I myght ete one morsell
I wold thynk the matter went very well

R

SYR. J.

Gossyp Jhān Jhān now mych good do it you
What chere make you there by the fyre

JHĀN.

Master p̄son I thank you now
I fare well now after myne own desyre

SYR. J.

What dost Jhān Jhān I the requyre

JHĀN.

I chafe the wax here by the fyre

TYB.

Here is good drynk and here is a good py

SYR. J.

We fare very well thankyd be our lady

TYB.

Loke how the kokold chafyth the wax that is hard
And for his lyfe daryth not loke hetherward

SYR. J.

What doth my gossyp

J.

I chafe the wax
And I chafe it so hard that my fyngers krakkes
And eke the smoke puttyth out my eyes two
I burne my face and ray my clothys also
And yet I dare nat say one word
And they syt laughyng yender at the bord

TYB.

Now by my trouth it is a prety Jape
For a wyfe to make her husband her ape
Loke of Jhān Jhān which maketh hard shyft
To chafe the wax to stop therwith the clyft

JHĀN.

Ye that a vengeaunce take ye both two
Both hym and the and the and hym also
And that ye may choke with the same mete
At the furst mursell that ye do ete

TYB.

Of what thyng now doth thou clatter
Jhān Jhān or wherof doth thou patter

JHĀN.

I thafe¹ the wax and make hard shyft
To stop herwith of the payll the ryftt

SYR. J.

So must he do Jhān Jhān by my father kyn
That is bound of wedlok in the yoke

JHĀN.

Loke how the pyld preest crammyth in
That wold to god he myght therwith choke

TYB.

Now master pson pleasyth your goodnes
To tell vs some tale of myrth or sadnes
For our pastyme in way of communycacyon

¹ = chafe.

SYR. J.

I am content to do it for our recreacyon
And of .iii. myracles I shall to you say

JHĀN.

What must I chafe the wax all day
And stond here rostyng by the fyre

SYR. J.

Thou must do somwhat at thy wyues desyre
I know a man which weddyd had a wyfe
As fayre a woman as euer bare lyfe
And within a senyght after ryght sone
He went beyond se and left her alone
And taryd there about a .vii. yere
And as he cam homeward he had a heuy chere
For it was told hym that she was in heuen
But when that he comen home agayn was
He found his wyfe and with her chyldren seuen
Whiche she had had in the mene space
Yet had she not had so many by thre
Yf she had not had the help of me
Is not this a myracle yf euer were any
That this good wyfe shuld haue chyldren so many
Here in this town whyle her husband shuld be
Beyond the se in a farre contre

JHĀN.

Now in good soth this is a wonderous myracle
But for your labour I wolde that your tacle
Were in a skaldyng water well sod

TYB.

Peace I say thou lettest the worde of god

SYR. J.

An other myracle eke I shall you say
Of a woman whiche that many a day
Had been wedded and in all that season
She had no chylde nother doughter nor son
Wherfore to saynt Modwin she went on pilgrimage
    And offered there a lyue pyg as is the vsage
Of the wyues that in London dwell
And through the vertue therof truly to tell
Within a moneth after ryght shortly
She was delyuered of a chylde as moche as I
How say you is not this myracle monderous[1]

JHĀN.

Yes in good soth syr it is maruelous
But surely after myn opynyon
That chylde was nother doughter nor son
For certaynly and I be not begylde
She was delyuered of a knaue chylde

TYB.

Peas I say for goddes passyon
Thou lettest syr Johans cōmunication

SYR. J.

The thyrde myracle also is this
I knewe a nother woman eke ywys
Whiche was wedded et within .v. monthis after
She was delyuered of a fayre doughter
As well formed in euery membre et ioynt
And as parfyte in euery poynt
As thou she had gone .v. monthis full to thende
Lo here is .v. monthis of aduantage

_____
[1] =wonderous.

JHĀN.

A wonderous myracle so god me mende
I wolde eche wyfe that is bounde in maryage
And that is wedded here within this place
Myght haue as quicke spede in euery such case

TYB.

Forsoth syr Johan yet for all that
I haue sene the day that pus my cat
Hath had in a yere kytlyns eyghtene

JHĀN.

Ye tyb my wyfe and that haue I sene
But howe say you syr Jhān was it good your pye
The dyuell the morsell that therof eate I
By the good lorde this is a pyteous warke
But nowe I se well the olde prouerbe is treu
The parysshe preest forgetteth yt euer he was clarke
But syr Jhān doth not remembre you
How I was your clerke et holpe you masse to syng
And hylde the basyn alway at the offryng
Yet neuer had halfe so good a clarke as I
But notwithstankyng[1] all this nowe our pye
Is eaten vp there is not lefte a byt
And you two together there do syt
Eatynge and drynkynge at your owne desyre
And I am Johan Jhān which must stāde by ye fyre
Chafyng the wax and dare none other wyse do

SYR J.

And shall we alway syt here styll we two
yt were to mych

T.

then ryse we out of this place

[1] = notwithstandyng.

SYR. J.

And kys me than in the stede of grace
And fare well leman and my loue so dere

JHĀN.

Cokkes body this waxe it waxte colde agayn here
But what shall I anone go to bed
And eate nothyng nother meate nor brede
I haue not be wont to haue such fare

TYB.

Why were ye not serued there as ye are
Chafyng the waxe standyng by the fyre

JHĀN.

Why what mete gaue ye me I you requyre

SYR. J.

Wast thou not serued I pray the hartely
Both with the brede the ale and the pye

JHĀN.

No syr I had none of that fare

TYB.

Why were ye no serued there as ye are
Standyng by the fyre chafyng the waxe

JHĀN.

Lo here be many tryfyls and knakkes
By kokkes soule they wene I am other drōke or mad

TYB.

And had ye no meate Johan Johan no had

JHĀN.

No tyb my wyfe I had not a whyt

TYB.

What not a morsell

J.

No not one byt

For honger I trowe I shall fall in a sowne

SYR. J.

O that were pyte I swere by my crowne

TYB.

But is it trewe

J.

Ye for a surete

TYB.

Dost thou ly

J.

No so mote I the

TYB.

Hast thou had nothyng

J.

No not a byt

TYB.

Hast thou not dronke

J.

No not a whyt

TYB.

Where wast thou

J.

By the fyre I dyd stande

TYB.

What dydyst

'J.'

I chafed this waxe in my hande
Where as I knewe of wedded men the payne
That they haue and yet dare not complayne
For the smoke put out my eyes two
I burned my face and rayde me clothes also
Mendyng the payle whiche is so rotten and olde
That it wyll not skant together holde
And syth it is so and syns that ye twayn
Wold gyue me no meate for my suffysaunce
By kokes soule I wyll take no lenger payn
Ye shall do all your self with a very vengaunce
For me and take thou there thy payle now
And yf thou canst mend it let me se how

TYB.

A horson knaue hast thou brok my payll
Thou shalt repent by kokkes lylly nayll
Rech me my dystaf or my clyppyng sherys
I shall make the blood ronne about his erys

JHĀN.

Nay stand styll drab I say and come no nere
For by kokkes blood yf thou come here
Or yf thou onys styr toward this place
I shall throw this shouyll full of colys in thy face

TYB.

Ye horson dryuyll get the out of my dore

JHĀN.

Nay get thy out of my house thou prestes hore

SYR. J.

Thou lyest horson kokold euyn to thy face

JHĀN.

And thou lyest pyld preest with an euyll grace

TYB.

And yu lyest

J.

Et yu lyest syr

[T.]

Et yu lyest agayn

JHĀN.

By kokkes soule horson preest thou shalt be slayn
Thou hast eate our pye and gyue me nought
By kokkes blod it shalbe full derely bought

TYB.

At hym syr Johan or els god gyue the sorow

JHĀN.

and haue at your hore et thefe[1] saynt george to borow

Here they fyght by the erys a whyle et than the
preest and the wyfe go out of the place

[1] = these.

JĦAN.

A syrs I haue payd some of them euen as I lyst
They haue borne many a blow with my fyst
I thank god I haue walkyd them well
And dryuen them hens but yet can ye tell
Whether they be go for by god I fere me
That they be gon together he and she
Vnto his chamber and perhappys she wyll
Spyte of my hart tary there styll
And peraduenture there he and she
Wyll make me cokold euyn to anger me
And then had I a pyg in the woyrs panyer
Therfore by god I wyll hye me thyder
To se yf they do me any vylany
And thus fare well this noble company.

FINIS

Imprynted by Wyllyam Rastell the .xii. day of February
the yere of our lord .M. .ccccc. and .xxxiii.

Cum priuilegio

APPENDIX

THE BIRTHPLACE OF JOHN HEYWOOD

(a) *London.*

Of the first school of thought, Bishop John Bale, author of *Index Britanniae Scriptorum*, who lived nearest to his time and whose testimony is to be noticed as he wrote himself several tragedies and interludes, calls him "civis Londiniensis." He writes of "Joannes Heyvode, *civis Londiniensis* musices ac rhythmicae artis in sua lingua studiosus; ingeniosus pro choreis post comessationem et epulas hilariter ducendis," etc., and having established the identity of Heywood gives the date presumably of his flourishing 1556. ("Vixit ille [anno] Domini 1556".)

The only doubt here is about the exact meaning of "civis Londiniensis."

(1) Does Bale mean that he was born in London, or that he lived in London? In his *Illustrium Majoris Britanniae Scriptorum Summarium*, fol. 235, dated 1548, he says: "Ioannes Heywode, ut Orpheus alter, instrumentorum studiosus, musicus et poeta magnam habebat in sua lingua gratiam. *Londini jam habitat ad senium festinans.*"

(2) Or does he refer only to the conferring of citizenship on John Heywood, "citizen and stacyoner of London and oon of the Kynges servauntes," 1523; when, as Dr. A. W. Reed points out, John Heywood was admitted to the freedom of London through the influence of Henry VIII? ("John Heywoode ys admitted into the liberties of this citie paying the old hanse.")

Dr. Reed alleges that Heywood did not claim admission by patrimony, and that therefore he was not born of London parents.

But Iohannes Pitseus (John Pitts), writing in 1619 in *De*

Rebus Anglicis, 1, 753, of Iohannes Hayuodus ("vir pius, utcumque doctus, valde ingeniosus musices quam vocalis quam instrumentalis peritus, elegans in poesi et plus quam credit potest in familiari colloquio lepidus atque facetus") says that he was *born in London*: ("Londini in Anglia natus") and that "in his old age he is said to have lived in London" ("Senex Londini vixisse dictur").

Similarly Antony à Wood in his *Athenae Oxonienses*, vol. i, 116, published 1691, which purports to be "an exact history of all the writers and bishops who have had their education in the most ancient and famous university of Oxford" from 1500 to 1690, says, "John Heywood or Heewood, a most noted poet and jester of his time, *was born in the city of London*, and notwithstanding he is said to be 'Civis Londinensis' (*sic*), yet he laid a foundation of learning in this university."

(b) North Mimms.

Of the second school of thought, Henry Peacham, in 1622, writes in the *Compleat Gentleman*, p. 95: "In the time of Edward VI lived merrie John Heywood who wrote his *Epigrammes*: as also Sir Thomas More his *Utopia* in the parish, wherein I was borne: where either of them *dwelt* and had faire possessions." He adds an explanatory note "North Mimmes in Herfordshire neere to St. Albanes."

The same writer in *Thalias's Banquet* in Epigram 80 writes with the same explanatory note:

> I thinke the place that gave me first my birth,
> The genius had of epigram and mirth;
> There famous Moore did his Utopia wright,
> And thence came Heywood's epigrams to light.

The Mores had been connected with the neighbourhood of Mimms for some time. More Hall, as it is now called, or Gobions (or Gubbins) was held by Sir Richard Gobions in Stephen's reign. But John More held the Manor in 1390, and may have helped to endow its fourteenth-century church;

and in 1397 "one knight's fee and a half" in North Mimms was held by John More of London. In 1500 it was held by Sir John More, father of Sir Thomas, the Lord Chancellor. The local story has it that he wrote *Utopia* there in 1516.

The story has it, too, that Henry VIII, the chief patron of Heywood, came down to Mimms.

We know from Pitseus that John Heywood was for many years very intimate with More ("multis annis familiarissimus"), and Thomas Stapleton in his *Life of More* about 1612 mentions in addition to John Clement and William Rastall among the friends of More, John Heywood ("Ioannes quoque Haiwodus quo per aliquot annos familiariter Thomas Morus usus fuerat"). Accordingly it is often asserted in the argument of Heywood's birthplace, that More helped Heywood and that the help was given at North Mimms.

Now More had written, *A mery jest how a sergeant would lerne to playe the frere* and *Nyne Pageauntes* also.

Erasmus wrote of him in his *Vita Thomae Mori* that "in his youth he wrote and acted in little comedies" ("Adolescens comediolas et scripsit et egit"). Some stress should be laid on the word "adolescens."

Again More had written verses and dialogues and epigrams very much in Heywood's style, and with some of his technique. "The apothegms of Sir Thomas Moor" are quoted by Jeremy Collier in his edition of 1688 (e.g. "He that is covetous when he is old is like a thief that steals when he is going to the gallows").

Again, More had written a Latin epigram[1] in Heywood's manner about *The Spider and the Fly*, which very much calls to mind Heywood's long allegory of *The Spider and the Flie*.

All this makes it at least plausible that More partially inspired Heywood's work and brought him out, and that they lived near each other.

Again, More was related not merely by common intel-

---

[1] Venatus Araneae (in the *Epigrammata Thomae Mori*, 1518).

lectual and religious outlooks, but by marriage to Heywood, and to Heywood's printers, the Rastalls. John Rastall had married Elizabeth, Sir Thomas More's sister, and according to à Wood wrote several interludes (e.g. *Natura Naturata*, "a large and ingenious comedy containing a description of three parts of the world") and a Dialogue "concerning Purgatory," in three books.

Lastly, as we shall see later, John Heywood later in life owned property at North Mimms. There is evidence that he bought the lease of a property there entitled "The Iveries" in November 1540. But there is no proof which I have been able to discover to-day, at North Mimms or St. Albans, or at Gobions, that Heywood had an interest in North Mimms before he acquired "The Iveries," or that he was born there.

(c) Stock.

Of the third school of thought Dr. Reed suggests in *The Library* of 1917 that the Heywoods were of yeoman stock, and that Stock Harvard, near Chelmsford, was their home. The evidence of William Heywood, "A yoman" who was associated partly with the Manor of "The Inge Gynge Joyberd Laundry," Hertford Stock (Essex), helps to explain a line in Heywood's play *The Wether*, which had hitherto baffled everyone. Dr. Reed from this and other remarkable evidence thinks it likely that Heywood was a yeoman of Stock in Essex.

There is a reference to a Heywood and *Essex* cheese-making in Barnaby Googe's *Foure Bookes of Hysbandry* (1601). But I can find few internal traces of the yeoman in Heywood's work. He seems to me to write far more as a townsman.

*   *   *   *   *

In conclusion, therefore, I think that the body of the evidence will accumulate to show that he must have been born near the Court, and probably at London.

INDEX